# Platonism in
# Recent Religious Thought

# Platonism in
# Recent Religious Thought

BY WILLIAM D. GEOGHEGAN

Columbia University Press

NEW YORK 1958

# Acknowledgments

I AM GRATEFUL to the following for permission to quote from the copyrighted material listed below.

The British Academy: W. R. Inge, "Origen."

Cambridge University Press: A. N. Whitehead, *The Concept of Nature; An Enquiry concerning the Principles of Natural Knowledge.*

The Clarendon Press, Oxford: A. E. Taylor, *A Commentary on Plato's Timaeus.*

Constable and Company, Ltd.: A. E. Taylor, *Plato.*

The Dial Press: A. E. Taylor, *Plato, the Man and His Work*, copyright, 1936.

E. P. Dutton & Company, Inc.: W. R. Inge, *Studies of English Mystics.*

The Library of Living Philosophers, Paul Arthur Schilpp, Editor: Vol. II, *The Philosophy of George Santayana;* Vol. III, *The Philosophy of Alfred North Whitehead.*

Longmans, Green & Co., Limited: W. R. Inge, *God and the Astronomers; Personal Idealism and Mysticism; The Philosophy of Plotinus*, Vols. I and II; *The Platonic Tradition in English Religious Thought.*

The Macmillan Company: J. H. Muirhead, ed., *Contemporary British Philosophy*, Second Series; A. E. Taylor, *Does God Exist?* copyright, 1947; A. N. Whitehead, *Adventures of Ideas*, copyright, 1933; *Process and Reality*, copyright, 1929; *Religion in the Making*, copyright, 1926; *Science and the Modern World*, copyright, 1925.

Macmillan and Co., Ltd., and St. Martin's Press, Inc.: A. E. Taylor, *The Faith of a Moralist*, Vols. I and II; *Philosophical Studies;* William Temple, *Christ the Truth; Mens Creatrix; Nature, Man and God.*

Methuen & Co., Ltd.: W. R. Inge, *Christian Mysticism.*

Thomas Nelson and Sons, Ltd.: A. E. Taylor and William Temple, articles in *Mind*, Gilbert Ryle, ed.

Oxford University Press: *European Civilization: Its Origin and Development*, Vol. VI, under the direction of Edward Eyre; W. R. Inge, Introduction to *The Essence of Plotinus*, comp. by G. H. Turnbull; F. S. Marvin, ed., *Recent Developments in European Thought*.

Peter Davies Limited: A. E. Taylor, *Socrates*.

The Philosophical Library, Inc.: A. N. Whitehead, *Essays in Science and Philosophy*.

Princeton University Press: P. E. More, *The Catholic Faith; Christ the Word; The Christ of the New Testament; The Demon of the Absolute; Pages from an Oxford Diary; Platonism; The Religion of Plato; The Sceptical Approach to Religion*.

G. P. Putnam's Sons: W. R. Inge, *Christian Ethics and Modern Problems*, copyright, 1930; P. E. More, *Shelburne Essays*, Sixth Series, copyright, 1909.

Routledge & Kegan Paul, Ltd.: F. M. Cornford, *Plato's Cosmology*.

Charles Scribner's Sons: A. E. Taylor, "Theism," in James Hastings, ed. *Encyclopaedia of Religion and Ethics*, Vol. XII; George Santayana, *The Idea of Christ in the Gospels; Interpretations of Poetry and Religion; The Life of Reason*, Vol. III; *Platonism and the Spiritual Life; Realms of Being; Soliloquies in England and Other Soliloquies*.

University of Chicago Press and Hutchinson and Co., Ltd.: W. R. Inge, *Mysticism in Religion*, copyright, 1948, by the University of Chicago; "The Permanent Influence of Neo-Platonism on Christianity," in *The American Journal of Theology*, now *The Journal of Religion*, copyright, 1900, by the University of Chicago.

Yale University Press: John Dewey, *A Common Faith*.

Brunswick, Maine                    WILLIAM D. GEOGHEGAN
May, 1957

# Contents

these different types have the common characteristic of representing serious and sustained thought about major religious ideas. Another aim of this book is to show that Platonism as a whole is concerned with five major ideas and their relations: God, the Ideal, natural existence, historical existence, and the nature and destiny of man's moral personality. Finally, it will be held that the ambiguities of Platonism arise from the nature of Platonism itself, from modifications of Platonism due to Christian or naturalistic interpretations, or from the impossibility of reaching conclusive answers to the questions under discussion.

We shall regard Inge, More, Taylor, Temple, Whitehead, and Santayana as individual thinkers, with attention paid to the origin, nature, and development of the thought of each in its historical and systematic forms. Secondly, these thinkers will be paired in terms of the principles on which they are in fundamental agreement. Thus, both Inge and More adopt what may be called the principle of the maximum assimilation of Platonic and Christian thought. However, since they differ sharply about the essential nature of Platonism and Christianity, their differences are well worth investigating. Taylor and Temple are paired because they tend toward a more limited assimilation of Platonic and Christian thought, and because both classical Christian and modern concepts are more influential in their thinking. Whitehead and Santayana are at one in being more naturalistic in their religious thought than the others. Both of them critically react from traditional Platonism and Christianity, and are more emphatic than the others in incorporating revised Platonic concepts into their thought. Thirdly, we shall inquire how these six individuals and the three types of thought which they represent are otherwise related to each other. Finally, we shall attempt to see Platonic religious thought as a whole.

In summary: this book takes the form of a critical exposition which seeks to answer the following questions about each thinker. (1) How and why did he come to be a Platonist? (2) What is his conception of the origin and nature of Platonism? (3) How is Platonism constructively and critically related to the rest of his religious thought, both explicitly and implicitly? (4) In his view, what is living and dead in Platonism? Where and upon what grounds must Platonism be corrected or supplemented by other doctrines if it is to be viable? (5) Finally, what may Platonism become?

# I: The Christian Platonism of W. R. Inge

WILLIAM RALPH INGE (1860–1954) was descended from a long line of English clergymen. He was educated at Eton and King's College, Cambridge, and was ordained Deacon in the Church of England in 1888 and Priest in 1890. As a classical tutor at Hertford College, Oxford (1889–1904), he began to search for a philosophy by which he could live. This he found in those Christian mystics who were steeped in the Platonic tradition, and in the thought of Plotinus.[1]

His two most notable contributions to religious thought are his Bampton Lectures of 1899, *Christian Mysticism*, and his Gifford Lectures at St. Andrew's in 1917–18, *The Philosophy of Plotinus*. Among his many writings on aspects of Platonism, the most relevant here is his Hulsean Lectures at Cambridge in 1925–26, *The Platonic Tradition in English Religious Thought*. This book provoked from Santayana his sympathetic yet astute critique, *Platonism and the Spiritual Life*. In *Christian Ethics and Modern Problems* and *God and the Astronomers* Inge deals with some of the problems thrown up by contemporary developments in the fields of the social and natural sciences. *Mysticism in Religion* (1947), Inge's summing-up of the central features of his thought, is a blend of Neo-Platonic and Christian mysticism, supplemented with elements from recent Indian and Russian religious thought. *The End of an Age*, written when he was eighty-seven, consists of essays on some of the more urgent practical problems of our times. His last work was *Diary of a Dean* (1950).

As Lady Margaret Professor of Divinity at Cambridge (1907–11) and as Dean of St. Paul's (1911–34), Inge attained prominence as one of the leading intellectual and spiritual lights in contemporary English religious thought. Although he has been called a Buddhist by Rashdall and a Quaker by Shaw,[2] he looks upon himself as a Christian Platonist on the right wing of theological liberalism. As such he does not sharply distinguish between philosophy and religion, but within the framework of Idealism aims to set forth a "religious philosophy" to which he may consecrate his life. Inge defines Idealism as the interpretation of the world, which consists of fact and value as inseparable correlatives, according to a scale of value, or Plato's Idea of the Good.[3] He accepts the idealistic criteria of experience and canons of knowledge such as coherence and purpose, while he avoids panlogism by emphasizing the surds or irrationals of existence.

Inge is primarily concerned with delineating the structure of the "spiritual world" in terms of Neo-Platonic and Christian mysticism and value theory. Christian Platonism today has two functions. It should not be regarded as an apologia for a lost cause, but it should be valued for its preservation of traditional values and for its creative potentialities for the future spiritual life of man. Only by means of this type of religious thought can the mind and heart of a contemporary Christian be satisfied and the decadence of the Christian faith forestalled.[4]

*Characteristic Doctrines of Christian Platonism.* In his polemic against the excessive temporalism of modernist philosophies Inge calls Christian Platonism, which upholds the doctrine of the eternal world, the *philosophia perennis.* In his efforts to vindicate absolute values and a rational universe against irrationalistic pragmatism and the fideism of Roman Catholic Modernism he calls it the Great Tradition.

With respect to the extremes of reductionist materialism and subjective idealism in cosmological speculation, Christian Platonism is a "real-idealism." Finally, it is the "religion of the Spirit," in contrast to Roman Catholic authoritarianism, Protestant obscurantism and antinomianism, and humanitarian sentimentalism.[5]

Since philosophy is defined as free inquiry into the ultimate nature and meaning of existence, Christian Platonism must begin at this point in order to protect itself against popular relativism. It is the cardinal postulate of Platonism that "the perfectly real is perfectly knowable." This supreme act of intellectual faith must not be confused with mere intellectualism, as in the optimistic Hegelian view that "the real is the rational."[6] For Platonism the real consists of values—"not unrealized ideals, but facts understood in their ultimate significance." They do not constitute a "ballet of bloodless categories" but an intelligible, spiritual world with which the Platonist lives in close and lively connection.[7]

Another distortion of Platonism is found in the popular dualistic interpretation. Both Plato and Plotinus sought to give a unified interpretation of all experience. Plotinus' summation of his polemic against the Gnostics, who disparaged the world of sense experience—"All things Yonder are also Here"—aptly expresses Platonism's view of the world as a "unity-in-duality." It is a fundamental Platonic belief that the visible is the vehicle of the invisible, the material of the spiritual. Since we are amphibians, we necessarily have a footing in the two worlds of eternity and time, mind and matter, spirit and flesh.[8] The Platonist does not believe in a "supramundane physics." The dualism between the natural and the supernatural is the heritage of a brittle religious orthodoxy which is a hindrance to the progress of scientific and philosophical thought because it denies the necessary postulate of the continuity of nature. While Christian Platonism has no conflict with natural science, its interest in nature is not primarily scientific. It is essentially an attitude of "tender reverence" which, while tending to make an allegory of events, is not a romantic sentimentality. Nature is an integral aspect of an intelligible whole which is viewed in a spirit of consecration in which "thought becomes passionate, the passions become cold."[9]

While Matter is not evil for Platonism, the Platonist who is not a dilettante is obliged to practice a sane and moderate asceticism. The harsh Orphic and Pythagorean ethical and metaphysical dualism, in which the body is regarded as the "tomb" of the soul, is not an ingredient of Christian Platonism. Asceticism is not a program for buffeting and scourging the body, but an inner discipline of the will and mind. For Christian Platonism the consecration of the self and the knowledge of God proceed *pari passu*, and the seeming unreality of God and the spiritual world must be attributed to the failure of self-discipline. By the same token, a sober trust in "earned religious experience" is warranted.[10]

This religious and ethical doctrine of "assimilation to God" indicates Platonism's fundamental epistemological position that "like alone sees its like" or, in the words of Plotinus, "the spiritual world is not outside Spirit."[11] That this relation between God and man is one of likeness and not one of identity is the basis of Inge's rejection of ontologism. On the other hand, since human nature is *capax deitatis*, the Barthian conception of God as *ganz Andere* is also rejected. Positively, this doctrine provides the basis for a necessary religious symbolism, since there must be a resemblance between the symbol and the thing symbolized.

Historically, Inge regards the role of Socrates in Platonism as negligible, and subordinates Plato to Plotinus in the Platonic tradition. Between Aristotle and Plotinus, Platonism was not represented by a first-class thinker, although Clement and Origen successfully founded Christian Plato-

nism.[12] With the exception of an early, brief article Inge
does not explore Augustine's Platonism, although he accepts his critique of Neo-Platonism based on the doctrine
of the Incarnation.[13] After Plotinus, the Platonic tradition
is carried on by the proponents of the religion of the Spirit
—the German mystics, the Cambridge Platonists, and the
English poets, especially Wordsworth. Inge draws a parallel
between the confusion of Origen's era and our own, and
adopts his view of salvation. Man's spirit can be made whole
through Socratic self-knowledge and self-discipline, Platonic rationalistic Idealism, Neo-Platonic value theory, and
the doctrine that "the inner light is the gift of God, not, as
the Stoics thought, 'what we can give ourselves.' "[14]

*The Philosophy of Plato.* Against Nietzsche and with Jae-
ger, Inge does not regard Plato as a "brilliant digression"
from Greek thought. But Plato was a Christian before
Christ. Negatively, the nocturnal council in *Laws* is the
prototype of the Inquisition. Positively, Platonism was a
*preparatio evangelica* in the broad sense of providing the
groundwork for an intimate affinity between Hellenism and
Christianity. Inge holds that in the millennium before
Christ a new and unique spiritual enlightenment entered
the world, and through the thought of Plato gained "a permanent foothold in the West." Essentially this consisted of
the doctrine that there is an unseen eternal world of which
the visible world is a pale copy.[15] Plato developed this doctrine, not as a "systematic philosopher," but as a poet and
prophet, and in such a way that he must be regarded as
"the father of European Mysticism."[16]

The evidence of Plato's mysticism can be seen in his in-
timacy with Socrates, whom Inge, following Taylor, regards as partly a mystic; in his contention in *Epistle* VII
that true philosophy is conveyed as a "leaping flame" from
teacher to disciple; and in the fact that Plotinus, a supreme

philosophical mystic, regards Plato as the authoritative source of his thought.[17] Parts of the *Timaeus, Republic, Symposium,* and *Phaedrus* (especially 245c and 249c) disclose the mystical quality of Plato's religious thought, both in his poetry and in his theory of Ideas.

Despite the fact that Plato ranked *to phantastikon* as the lowest faculty of the soul, he was a superlative prose-poet. His myths may be divided into three classes. (1) Inge regards the use of the "pious fraud" or "medicinal lie" as unscrupulous. (2) The "likely tale," as in *Timaeus, Gorgias,* or *Republic,* which is used to illuminate some obscurity of cosmology or theodicy, Inge regards as legitimate. Like More and Santayana, he holds poetry to be "the natural language of religion."[18] (3) Finally, some of Plato's myths are ambiguous, and lend themselves to dangerously divergent interpretations. Such is the myth of the charioteer and the two steeds in the *Phaedrus.* Here two views of Nature are suggested, one of which leads to the healthy ascetic view that Nature is the germ of vehicle of the higher life, while the other regards Nature as the opponent of reason in the moral struggle, thus giving rise to a harsh dualism.[19]

The central point at which Plato's philosophical, religious, and poetic interests converge is the famous doctrine of the Ideas. Inge deplores, on the one hand, Plato's tendency to hypostatize static, abstract concepts, while on the other hand, he objects to the dynamic version of Ideas in the *Sophist.* The valid source of Plato's theory of Ideas is the "visualism" which comes spontaneously to the natural or personal Platonist. It is, as Pater puts it, "a sensuous love of the unseen" which regards Ideas as "creative values" universally putting forth "organic filiaments."[20]

There are three major misinterpretations of Plato's Ideas. The first is that of Aristotle, who was correct in saying that Plato thought Ideas were "separate" from particulars, but wrong in thinking that Plato regarded Ideas as "separate *things.*" Secondly, the "psychologism" of Natorp and Stewart, in making *ta noeta* depend upon *ta aistheta*, is an unwarranted modernization of Plato. Finally, while Bolzano and Taylor are correct in insisting that an Idea is not a process of thinking but an object of thought, they do not give due weight to the possibility that Plato held that Ideas were "thoughts of God."[21]

Inge observes that Plato does not finally set over against one another in irreconcilable opposition the two worlds of *stasis* and *kinesis,* as the discussion of the *gene* in the *Sophist* shows. Plato's repudiation of metaphysical dualism is paralleled by his rejection of other forms of dualism, which some interpreters nonetheless saddle upon him, by regarding matter as evil, or by supposing that an "evil world-soul" operates in opposition to the Demiurge. In the last analysis, however, Inge finds Plato's religious thought deficient in two major respects. His position in the history of mysticism is less firm than that of Plotinus, because the latter unified doctrines which Plato tentatively threw out. Secondly, while Plato saw that the root of sin lay in self-will and that man cannot get rid of moral evil without pain (thus anticipating Christian teaching), he was essentially overoptimistic. But beyond this, Inge prizes Plato's faith in reason and his reasonable faith. Whether in opposition to Sophistic *misologia* or against contemporary equivalents, the intellectual courage which Plato manifested is a permanently valuable achievement of the human spirit.[22]

*The Religious Thought of Plotinus.* With respect to the interpretation of Neo-Platonism in general and the thought of Plotinus in particular, Inge completely reverses himself. At the turn of the century he asked why Christianity won, and Neo-Platonism lost, the battle between them. But in his Gifford Lectures he finds that Neo-Platonism resisted Christianity and was apparently defeated, but actually survived in Christian thought. Far from being a deviation from the orthogenesis of classical thought—"swooning away in a cloud of gas"—Neo-Platonism is the consummation of "the longest period of unimpeded thinking which the human race has yet been permitted to enjoy."[23]

Plotinus was not only a supreme mystic, but a thinker whose *Enneads* present a rich, complex, and distinctive world view upon a rational basis. This world view involves four major postulates. The first is that of a hierarchy of knowledge, ranging from the "kind of bastard reasoning" which knows Matter, through dialectic, to the intuition of *ta noeta* by *nous* and of *to Hen* by *nous eron*. Secondly, it involves hierarchies of existence and value which are believed to correspond ultimately. The difficulty here is that existence is monistic ("there are no minus signs") while values are both positive and negative. Thirdly, this world view involves the doctrine of the "one-sided dependence" of the lower aspects of existence upon the higher. "The lower needs the higher; the higher is complete without the lower." Finally, Plotinus views reality as a spectrum in which the colors are not absolutely distinct, but rather continually merge into each other.[24]

On the basis of these postulates Inge sees Plotinus concerned with establishing three truths: that of a spiritual reality against Stoic and Epicurean materialism, that of a realistic epistemology against Academic scepticism and eclecticism, and that of the "unity, goodness, and sacredness of the universe" against the Gnostics.[25] The first and third truths are involved in Plotinus' conception of the *kosmos aisthetos* and the *kosmos noetos*. The phenomenal world, which includes the *psyche*, has no *ousia* in itself, being derived from and dependent upon the intelligible world. The world of appearance may be regarded either as an imperfect vision or as an imperfect copy of the intelligible world. It differs from its archetype in presenting us with diversity unreconciled with unity (*hen kai polla*) instead of the complex unity (*plethos hen*) of *nous*, with mutual exclusion instead of "compenetration," with opposition instead of harmony, and with perpetual flux instead of the unchanging activity of *nous*. The thought of Plotinus thus excludes both the Gnostic pessimism and dualism, and Stoic materialistic monism. His "real-idealism" holds that the visible world is a beautiful image of the invisible, and he provides a permanently valuable refutation of reductionist materialism by indicating the contribution of the observer's mind to his knowledge of Nature.[26]

But Plotinus' own doctrine of Matter is vitiated by an equivocation stemming from his identification of the scales of value and existence. On the one hand, he holds that Matter is a relative term, and calls it immaterial (*asomatos*), indeterminate, and "no thing," but not "absolutely nothing." This view can be reconciled with the rest of his thought, and with the doctrines of Plato and Aristotle. On the other hand, when Plotinus speaks of Matter as "the nature (*phusis*) which resists Form," he poses the problem of evil in insoluble form.[27] Plotinus is more successful in dealing with Nature, whose life is an "upward striving" (*ephesis*) resulting from the confluence of the activity of the World Soul and Matter. Thus, there is no such thing as dead, inert Nature; it is all ensouled, for the creative *logoi* permeate it completely. While Plotinus' panpsychistic doctrine of "eternal creation" is free from the difficulties which attach to the Christian doctrine of *creatio ex nihilo* and to the mythical Demiurge of the *Timaeus*, it does not explain how *nous* can be "before" Matter, and yet be inoperative unless it has Matter to work upon.[28]

Inge finds two of Plotinus' cosmological conceptions to be of permanent value. First, Plotinus justified natural science as the study of extension, and hence of order and limitation (*taxis* and *peras*), which corresponds to the pursuit of the civic virtues in the *scala perfectionis*. Secondly, Time which is characterized by *ephesis* and succession means for Plotinus "the form of willed change." Time is a teleological category, and is the interval between the inception and consummation of the process in which a distinct Idea "There" becomes a finite purpose "Here."[29] This theory elaborates Plato's doctrine that Time is objectively, but not ultimately, real.

Inge's central concern with the *Enneads* is to show how they provide a rational basis for a mystical Idealism. The greatest advance which Plotinus made upon his Platonic predecessors is his doctrine that the soul is "itself transformed in its passage from darkness to light."[30] What Plotinus meant by *Psyche* is what we mean today by "Life." As he says, " 'It binds extremes together,' " in that it is an intermediary between appearance and reality. In modern idealism the self tends to be the "fixed centre" of the cosmos, while for Plotinus it is "the wanderer of the metaphysical world." *Psyche* differs from *nous* chiefly in that it is localized and is characterized by unfulfilled desire. Yet the Universal Soul as "the life of the world" plays the theistic roles of Creator and Providence. It is truly universal, yet not incarnate in the world. This is a doctrine of "panentheism" which is compatible with contemporary biologically oriented thought, and incompatible with any dualistic "bifurcation of nature." So far as individual souls are concerned, the same soul is both Here and There. "Here" it is separated from other souls; "There" it is a distinct individual, yet there is no barrier between any other soul and it. For Plotinus each soul is genuinely teleological—"The true being— the distinctness—of each individual consists in its *raison d'être (to dia ti)*."[31]

Sensation, imagination, and the ego are those aspects of psychic life which are especially relevant to religious thought. Sensation is based upon the soul's "faint sympathy" with all of life, which enhances the sense of the unity of Nature. "The difference between sensations and spiritual perceptions is one of degree; sensations are dim spiritual perceptions, spiritual perceptions are clear sensations." Thus, Nature and Spirit are a "unity-in-duality." Plotinus' estimate of *to phantastikon* is higher than Plato's, since he assigns it to the discursive reason. His doctrine of *nous eron* is comparable to Wordsworth's interpretation of imagination as "reason in her most exalted mood." This Inge regards as the key to the creation of religious symbols, and the means of preserving them from evaporation or petrifaction.[32]

What we today call self-consciousness Plotinus would have called inattention. The root of this anti-mystical conception lies in our predilection to attribute a primary importance to the abstract ego. This concept involves the rigid opposition of ego and non-ego, the supposition that the ego is identical through time, and the confused notion that the ego is both one's self and one's property. Plotinus, on the contrary, points out that there is mutual intercourse between subject and object on the psychic level, not to speak of a complete lack of barriers in the *kosmos noetos*. Secondly, consciousness itself "accrues" (*gignetai*), as the individual strives after unity and universality. Thirdly, he has no trace of what has come to be a burdensome heritage of Western thought—the "proprietary" notion of selfhood. While Plotinus holds individuality to be a fact (*dei hekaston hekaston einai*), the question whether it is *my* self which is "There" is meaningless for him. Man is potentially all things, and Plotinus' classifications of him as "double" or "threefold" must be regarded as heuristically fluid.[33]

The *psyche* is essentially fluid, and the end of its process of transformation is indicated in three closely related concepts: immortality, the reciprocal operation of *nous* and *noesis* as correlatives, and the ascent to the One. Plotinus' concept of immortality provides a connecting link between

psychic life "Here" and the *nous en psyche* "There." Since
man is a compound being of Body and Soul, and since the
Body obviously perishes, it is only the Soul which can
abide. But the Soul as such does not endure, only the *nous
en psyche*. This optimistic view of a pure, immortal center
of the soul is of considerable historical interest, since it contains the root of the mystical doctrine of *synderesis* and of
Boehme's *Fünklein*. Plotinus is at one with Spinoza in holding that the desire for immortality is not motivated by a
thirst for external rewards and fear of punishment: "If any
man seeks in the good life anything beyond itself, it is not
the good life which he is seeking."[34]

Plotinus' epistemology is not a subjective idealism because *nous* does not create *ta noeta*. It is not a transcendental
idealism because the intelligible world is not outside of
mind. It is not a dualism because *nous* and *ta noeta* are not
opposed as subject and object. Positively, *nous* and *ta noeta*
constitute a "real-idealism." The *eide* link thought and
thing, and *nous* creates the cosmos as known by *dianoia*, as
well as the reason which knows it. For Plotinus the Ideas
are essentially absolute, eternal, creative values. Man could
not rationally pursue values noncoincident with individual
advantage unless ultimate reality were supra-personal. Since
his psychophysical ego is an object for every man, he must
be more than it, and so be able to achieve spirituality, which
Inge defines as "a persistent attitude of mind, which will
never be immersed in the particular instance."[35]

We are now prepared to confront the ultimate doctrine
of Plotinus' religious thought, that "we can know the un-
knowable, because in our deepest ground we are the un-
knowable." The vision of the One is reached by the three
major paths of dialectic, perfection, and mysticism. The ultimate rational justification of the One lies in the fact that
neither *nous* nor *ta noeta* can be reduced to the other, despite the fact that they are inseparable: the One underlies

both. Furthermore, since both *nous* and *ta noeta* are multiple, neither could be the One. The path of dialectic discovers that the One has certain distinctive characteristics. In the first place, it is not a number, a bare unit. Rather it is comparable to the Pythagorean Monad, the undifferentiated whole, from which the notion of discerptibility is excluded. Secondly, the One is the "First Cause." This doctrine is unaffected by the objection that the causal regress is infinite, and does not undertake to explain how plurality can emanate from unity. It holds that while all values and existences are bound together in a continuous chain, the One is that which is independent, and that upon which all else depends.[36]

In his ethical life man aspires toward the One as Final Cause. The Good (*to agathon*) is teleological, but not merely moral. Virtue for Plotinus is *a* good. The Good for him, says Inge, is "unity as the goal of desire." Thus, it is well called the Perfect, since " 'it needs nothing.' " Plotinus' ethical theory is a high-minded but conventional heritage of the classical tradition. Two outstanding Platonic features are found in his doctrine of "assimilation to God" as the true motive of the ethical life, and in his fundamental contrast between true and false standards of values. Against Whittaker, who holds that Plotinus was a determinist, Inge maintains that he was a believer in human freedom since he asserts the reality of final causes. The chief defects of Plotinus' ethics lie in the premium put on the motive of invulnerability and the moral isolation of the Neo-Platonic saint. Proclus' doctrine of indivisible goods is closer to the Christian view that souls depend upon each other for the achievement of their perfection.[37]

The roots of Plotinus' mysticism are to be found in Plato. In an isolated but influential passage (*Republic* 509b) Plato placed the Good beyond essence and existence. Neo-Platonism went forward with this view, holding that while we can form no idea of the One, we are not cut off from it. Nevertheless, Plotinus tells us too much about the absolutely transcendent, with the result that his successors postulate a more ineffable somewhat behind it. When commentators overemphasize the One as transcendent rather than regarding it as "the Unity underlying and transcending all plurality," they misrepresent Plotinus as the apostle of acosmism in the Western world. Inge rejects this interpretation because for Plotinus the mystical path is one of discipline of the whole man in which knowledge and experience proceed *pari passu* under the guidance of dialectic. The " 'higher reason is king,' " and to aspire to rise above it is to fall outside it. Secondly, Plotinus is not acosmistic because he includes the "civic virtues" in the purgative stage of the *scala perfectionis*. Pursuit of these virtues inculcates the order and limitation which are also attributes of the divine nature. Finally, many commentators fail to observe Plotinus' distinction between the One (or Godhead) and the Great Spirit (or God). This leads them to ignore "the whole rich world of supersensuous reality which is the spiritual home of the Platonist." Consequently, the nihilism which frequently infects Indian mysticism is erroneously attributed to Plotinus. *Nous eron* craves and attains a vision of the One *and* the vision of the world of Platonic Ideas. The Sage knows that there is "nothing between" his *nous en psyche* and the One, but his spiritual life is lived in the "intelligible world."[38]

Inge observes that Plotinus' description of ecstasy is not merely biographical, since it agrees with the witness of many other mystics. He also cautions against exaggerating the magnitude of the role of *ekstasis* in the *Enneads*. The process of inner simplification (*haplosis*) has much in common with the *via negativa* trodden by many other mystics. It is an intense concentration upon essentials and not "a progressive impoverishment of experience until nothing is left."

It is the systole of the spiritual life, necessary for its later expansion in the world of Ideas, and identification with the One. Plotinus' mysticism is remarkably free from adventitious and pathological symptoms, such as occultism, self-manipulation, and the experience of dereliction. His type of mysticism, which is the quest of a "state" rather than a "person," affords a superior disinterestedness of spirit, despite the fact that a state is not as clear a goal as a person.[39]

Inge agrees with Bosanquet that Neo-Platonic religious thought can be summed up in the doctrine of the vision of God as the eternal source and standard of values. Christian religious thought is most compatible with this, while it is not at all compatible with Epicureanism, Persian dualism, modern pluralism, and agnosticism. The religious thought of Plotinus is what Platonism properly came to be. Inge agrees with Troeltsch that the synthesis of Neo-Platonism and New Testament Christianity is "the only possible solution of the problem of the present day" and that it will "once more be dominant in modern thought."[40]

*Critical Remarks on Inge's Conception of Platonism.* Inge does not provide a clear, critical definition of Platonism, but simply gives examples of why he thinks it must be regarded as a distinctive form of religious thought. His amorphous conception of Platonism is accounted for by his failure to achieve a synopsis of the tradition as a whole. Thus he defines the Platonic tradition as "the actual historical development of the school of Plato," which would make the Academics of the third century A.D. genuine Platonists. But this definition would exclude Plotinus himself, who was sedulous in avoiding the label "Academic" in favor of the term "Platonist."[41] Again he becomes enmeshed in an ambiguity because he fails to distinguish clearly between Platonism and Aristotelianism. On the one hand, he regards the *philosophia perennis* as the best of classical philosophy in a Christian form, while on the other hand he sharply separates the thought of contemporary Thomists from his own "Christianized Platonism." The most extreme consequence of this ambiguity is that he erroneously supposes that he is the only contemporary Christian Platonist.[42]

Generally, Inge regards the role of Socrates in the Platonic tradition as a trivial and negligible one. Only belatedly, and following Taylor, does he correct this distortion. Inge's treatment of Plato's life and thought is brief, perfunctory, and highly unoriginal. Its chief weakness lies in the fact that it regards Plato merely as a milestone along the road to Neo-Platonism, and makes Plotinus the normative, systematic Platonic thinker. Inge's depreciation of Plato's systematic thought arises from the fact that he does not recognize that Plato's thought gains its coherence not from the uniform answers given to problems, but from its many-angled attacks upon the same important problems. Plato's many discussions of the Ideas illustrate this point perfectly. Because Inge does not recognize this he uncritically condemns Plato for regarding the Ideas as static on the one hand, and as dynamic on the other. Actually, Plato's thought on the subject appears to have undergone a course of development, stimulated by continual criticism. Inge is not primarily concerned to find out what Plato meant by Ideas. Without a thorough critical understanding of their nature, he adapts them as "creative values" so that they may play a congenial role in his thought.

Inge is inconsistent on the question of the relation of God and the Idea of the Good. On the one hand, he says that what Plato meant by the Idea of the Good is identical with Nicholas Cusanus' definition of God as *valor valorum*. On the other hand, he adopts Taylor's argument that Plato's God is a *psyche* and not a Form, and consequently cannot be identified with the Idea of the Good.[43] Again, Inge finds Plato incompletely theistic because he was so vague about

God, and held that the *paradeigma* were metaphysically prior to deity. Elsewhere he contends that the *Timaeus* preserves the doctrine of the transcendence of God. Inge is not aware of these inconsistencies, hence does not try to reconcile them. He is so eager to apply Platonic conceptions for illustrative purposes that he does not give those conceptions adequate study. While Inge does not fall into the dualistic stereotype in interpreting Plato, and while he does something to indicate the religious quality of his thought, his contribution to our knowledge of Plato is both superficial and negligible because it is uncritical and unoriginal.

Inge's treatment of the thought of Plotinus is inadequate. Plotinus devotes much of the Sixth *Ennead* to a defense of Plato's *gene* against Aristotle's. Calling these mere "dialectical puzzles," Inge ignores them, and thus presents a truncated Plotinus. This neglect is all the more inexcusable since Inge commends Aliotta's defense of the Platonic categories as really fundamental and essential to the thinkableness of any experience.[44] Inge's translation of Plotinus' *nous*, *noeta*, and *noesis* as spirit, spiritual, and intuition is quite misleading. The words "intelligence" and "intelligibles" (Mackenna) better convey the rationalism of Plotinus and his affinity with Plato, while Inge's translation connotes an Oriental spiritualism. Again, where Plotinus held the infinity of the One to be a *fundamentum* of thought and reality, Inge speaks of a "postulate of faith."[45]

The major weakness of Inge's presentation of Plotinus lies in his failure to grasp the essence of Neo-Platonism as a whole, and to interpret the *Enneads* in that light. His book is a collection of topical essays rather than a unified treatment. As in his discussions of Plato, he is not primarily concerned with making clear what Plotinus meant. Thus, *ta noeta* again become "creative values" and the fundamental problems concerning their substantial reality are neglected. Inge provides us with no clear conception of the relation of

Plato and Plotinus, except to point out obvious affinities. He is content to assert that Neo-Platonism is the consummation of the thought of Plato, while he does not analyze adequately the Aristotelian and Stoic elements in Plotinus, and show their compatibility or incompatibility with Platonism. If Inge's interpretation of Plotinus be accepted, what is actually a pagan, rationalistic, naturalistic, and mystical philosophy is transformed into a genteel, post-Victorian Quakerism. Compared to the *Enneads* themselves and to such an interpretation of Neo-Platonism as is found in Whittaker's book, Inge obscures rather than clarifies the thought of Plotinus. He has not kept himself out of his subject to the degree which authoritative commentary requires. It is only in comparison with More's almost complete distortion of Neo-Platonism that Inge's work has scholarly merit.

*The Amalgam of Christian Platonism in Mysticism.* Inge points out that Neo-Platonism and Christianity share a common spirituality marked by detachment from the world and inwardness of spirit. They agree in distinguishing between a "higher" and a "lower" self, and hold that through Love man may grow in communion with an eternally perfect God and spiritual world. Historically, Platonic Idealism has been the "loving nurse" of Christian mysticism. In the religion of the Spirit Inge sees a firm and continuous tradition combined with fresh and vital possibilities, and tries to balance his traditional Christian Platonism with liberal and modernist elements. Thus he regards "religious experience" as the primary source of religious knowledge. This is synonymous with mystical experience, and does not involve reliance upon such questionable phenomena as auditions and visions. This doctrine does not base religious knowledge upon "pure feeling," which cannot, unlike eternal values, define the object of dependence. The sharpest contrast to Inge's doctrine is to be seen in the imposition of an external and infallible authority upon the inner freedom of the mystic, whether through ecclesiasticism or bibliolatry. Positively, religious experience undistorted by the foregoing vagaries is inwardly true and publicly verifiable because mystics agree upon the essentials of their widespread experiences.[46] When faith, reason, and worship are harmoniously combined they produce a form of religious knowledge which is both unitive and intuitive.

Inge defines Faith as "the resolution to stand or fall by the noblest hypothesis. It begins as an experiment and ends as an experience."[47] Its typical expression in Christian Platonism is found in Clement of Alexandria. Reason must be conjoined with faith because objective reality determines thought about it, and if we do not have reason as the criterion by which to test subjective feelings of what benefits us religion will become an intellectually groundless velleity. Revelation is the divine supplement to the reasonable faith which is the basis of worship. Its three major sources are in the *logos* or intelligible structure of Nature, in Christ's "transvaluation of values," and in the "inner light." Revelation refers to the disclosure of divine truth which man could not have discovered by himself but which, when once manifest, he recognizes in its true nature. Thus natural and revealed are not antithetical, but complementary, terms.[48]

Inge defines mysticism as "the attempt to realise the presence of the living God in the soul and in nature." Christian Platonism shows how this way of life may reach fruition. First, it assumes that man has a *psyches aisthesis* (Proclus), a means of discerning spiritual truth which is as authoritative in its sphere as the sense organs are in their sphere. A second necessary assumption consists of a combination of the Platonic epistemological principle that like alone knows like, its anthropological principle that man is a microcosm, and the Christian dogma that man is created *in imago dei*. Thirdly, Love is the ultimate link between man and God. Inge does not make a sharp distinction between *Agape* and *Eros;* even the contradiction between love as radical interest and as disinterestedness is merely verbal. Plotinus' *nous eron* and Spinoza's *amor intellectualis dei* illustrate how the two may be combined. Finally, Platonic mysticism receives its distinctive Christian character through the doctrine of the *unio mystica* with the Christ who is at once indwelling and a cosmic principle, the exemplar and fountain of divine love. At this point Christian devotional mysticism reaches its peak.[49]

Historically, there has been a great cleavage between devotional and speculative mysticism, although both are necessary as the systole and diastole of the spiritual life. If the former aspect is overemphasized, speculative mysticism tends to become dissolved in a fog of introspection and pantheism. Thus, the *via negativa* of Pseudo-Dionysius the Areopagite would one-sidedly exclude Nature as a valuable religious symbol by making it a burden to be escaped. His pantheistic identification of God with the universe is inferior to theism because it cannot distinguish between what is and what ought to be. This double error is reflected in Edward Caird's misleading definition of mysticism as the absorption of the human soul in God.[50]

While speculative mysticism has been subject to animistic perversions, in its proper theoretical function it is concerned with the nature of symbols and sacrament, the human soul, and God. Its basic position is that Nature is a symbol of God. Since man is an amphibian who ought to be properly related to the temporal and the eternal (as well as other contrasted, fundamental aspects of the world), he needs such a "bridge" as symbols afford. Religious symbolism is the expression of universal and ideal meanings through natural forms for the purpose of evoking insight. A great value of the doctrine of the "sacramental universe" is its discouragement of *Mysticismus*. A healthy and objective religious view of Nature can be seen in the Cambridge Platonists, and in Wordsworth, who emphasized the immanence of God in the contact of the human soul with Nature.[51]

The Christian Platonist view of human personality combines the Socratic-Platonic view of the *psyche* as the real self, Christianity's stern and tragic view that the soul may be lost, and the metaphysically fluid conception of Plotinus. Its antithesis is to be found in contemporary Personal Idealism, which holds that each self is a permanent and indiscerptible substance. This rigid view of the self tends to promote the error made current by Bradley and Taylor when they failed to recognize the reciprocal relation between self-enrichment and self-expenditure in the achievement of ideal ends. Inge defines personality as "the union of individuality and universality in a single manifestation." The Platonic ideal of integration ("a man ought to become one") entails a unification of the whole man, who is always in the making, and never a finished product. Although the postulate of the unity of personality is necessary for all thought, this does not mean that self-consciousness is the measure of personality. Such a view leads to "spiritual isolation" among selves, and obscures man's status as an organic factor of the universe. Although human personality is a very inadequate symbol for God, such personalistic terms as alienation and communion serve to express the relation between man and God.[52]

Inge uses the conception of panentheism to preserve equally the divine immanence with respect to man and the world along with the divine transcendence. One of his favorite metaphors to express this relation is that of a playwright to his plays: while his plays express the author's character, they are not the necessary conditions of his existence. On the basis of Plotinus' One as the Absolute, Inge defines Theism as the doctrine that "the ultimate ground of the universe is a single supreme Being who is perfect and complete in Himself."[53] The world which is perpetual, boundless, regular, and rational reflects the mind of the Creator who is eternal, infinite, changeless, and all-wise. Rejecting the theistic argument *a contingentia mundi*, he agrees with Lotze that the alternative to positing the existence of a single, creative First Cause is "intolerable." One alternative to panentheism is that form of contemporary pantheism which makes the world as necessary to God as God is to it. The essential characteristic of the naturalistic divinities of Croce, Gentile, Bergson, Alexander, Carr, and Whitehead is that God is subordinated to temporal process. Consequently, if the Law of Entropy rightly holds that Time is irreversible, these divinities will perish. The alternative of a finite God seems a justifiable inference from the facts of moral experience. But the God of Mill, Rashdall, and Wells is religiously inadequate. Unless God is the source of all reality, and that reality consists of absolute and eternal values, man has no satisfactory rational assurance for his religious venture of unreserved devotion.[54]

*The Amalgam of Christian Platonism in Value Theory.* Along with mysticism, the second great basis of the religion of the Spirit is value theory. Although Inge credits Kant and subsequent German axiologists with having given the development of value theory a salutary impetus in modern thought, he contends that the thought of Plato and Plotinus was essentially concerned with values. Values are religiously significant because they make up a world in which and through which God is revealed. Values are as coercive of recognition as facts because they, too, are given in experience; and value judgments are as valid as judgments based upon sense perception. Analysis of the familiar triad of ultimate values discloses that they are absolute and suprapersonal, objective and creative, and eternal.

There are two major criteria of the absoluteness of Goodness, Truth, and Beauty. While their interrelations must be expressed metaphorically, each is an end in itself and not a means to anything else, including other absolute values. Hence such claimants for the title as pleasure and life, which are sometimes foregone for the sake of other ends, are not absolute. These values are supra-personal because aspiration towards them inspires disinterestedness in men. They have an ineluctable attraction for those who, in their love for them, find their highest and deepest selves. It is vitally important to acknowledge the objective reality of values. They are not mere illusions or pure ideals. Santayana's Romantic Platonism posits a harsh dualism of value and existence and confuses imagination, which is the "objectifying contemplation" of the Platonists, with poetic fancy. As creative "Energies" values are *teleoi* with real cosmic status. But since they are not for any given man a possession, rather objects of aspiration, they may be regarded in the conventional sense as ideals.[55]

Inge regards the problem of the relation of value and existence as the central and perhaps insoluble problem of contemporary religious thought. His proposed solution is that reality is comprised of an unity-in-duality of value and existence. Ultimately they are identical, but actually there is a cleavage between values and the frame of Time and Space through which we apprehend them. Value and existence are to be distinguished, but not divorced, from one another because they interpenetrate in actuality, and their divorcement is as unfortunate as their premature identification. The divorce of existence and value amounts to a denial of Platonism's postulate of a rational universe, for it constitutes the basic assumption of an irrationalistic nominalism or pragmatism. The premature identification of fact and worth, as in Spencer's optimistic naturalism, bears a superficial resemblance to Plotinus' world view. However,

Spencer is driven to the position, as Plotinus is not, that something is better for having happened. Among the difficulties in the way of accepting the doctrine of inevitable and endless progress is that of ascertaining and applying a single, suitable criterion of progress, and the lack of any convincing evidence which is not cancelled by contrary facts. It is the decay of belief in the eternal world which has caused modern thought to commit itself to temporalism and futurism.

Clock-time, or "the measure of motion in space," has been correctly analyzed by Plato and Newton. Bergson's *durée* is sundered from space, and is without "direction." In his departure from the positions of Plato and Plotinus by identifying being with becoming, Bergson makes Time valueless. Platonism correctly regards Time and Space as the real, but not ultimately real, framework for man's relation with the eternal world. Against Alexander's "Gnostic syzygy" of Space-Time, Inge says that the assumption that the evolution of the species is "the primary law of the macrocosm is the extreme of provincialism," and that Alexander is unable to explain the origin of value. In direct opposition to modernism the Great Tradition posits a realm of eternal values of which temporal and spatial events are symbolic reflections or copies. Thus, in the Epistle to the Hebrews we have delineated the Judaeo-Christian-Platonic belief that temporal events are relevant to the eternal order. But historical happenings cannot "deflect" that order, and so are not of ultimate significance. The created world of Nature and History is an irreducible fact, but it cannot be an ultimate fact because it is not intelligible in itself.[56]

Man can know eternal values because he has an *ephesis* towards them. If this aspiration reaches fruition, they are immediately intuited. Man can become mentally identified with eternal values, and thus attain eternal life. In his earlier thought, Inge drew a sharp distinction between *aidios*, or everlasting duration, and *aionios*, or eternal, "a word of quality or value." On this basis he rejects the notion of personal immortality as durational because it gives rise to indefensibly grotesque imagery. At no time does he hold that there is a convincing proof of immortality. However, in his later thought he drops his former sharp distinction, holding that "duration cannot be excluded from our view of reality." Hence eternal values are known by temporal images, as well as by direct intuition.[57]

The role of absolute values in contemporary thought may be validated by discursive reason. Beauty ("the expression of a true idea under an appropriate form") is clearly the supreme intrinsic value, since it serves very few practical uses in human life. So far as Truth is concerned, Platonism and Christianity agree on a doctrine of reasonable faith. They repudiate any form of anti-intellectualism which denies the universality and objectivity of Truth. They hold that Truth is "the correspondence of idea with fact." They reject Naturalism (by which Inge means the reductionist materialism of T. H. Huxley and company) but have no conflict with the natural sciences. The latter are based upon such value judgments as faith in the order of Nature, and are an indispensable cathartic of religious fantasies. Following Plotinus, Inge refuses to moralize the Good. Platonism and Christianity agree that human happiness depends upon the correct standard of values, and that the moral will connects the psychic and spiritual planes in seeking to overcome the cleavage between "is" and "ought." They agree that ethics and religion are inseparable. As moral conduct should be a sacrament of the eternal world, so "religion in its highest form is an attempt to express reality sacramentally by living in harmony with it."[58] Apart from the difference which belief in Christ's revelation of God makes, Plato and St. Paul agree in teaching that man's soul is the normal self, but not the ideal self. They differ in their conceptions of the higher and lower parts of human nature. Platonism holds that the real man belongs to the eternal world, and that his body is a temporary and inferior adjunct. While St. Paul's "Spirit" is much the same as the Platonic *nous*, the "flesh" is not the human physical organism but a moral term, meaning "the lower instincts erected into a principle of life and action." The body is not evil.[59]

Christian Platonism must face the problem of evil because of the difficulty the reality of sin affords a reasonable faith. Earlier Inge called the Neo-Platonic and Augustinian conception of evil as "mere privation" an aesthetic and irreligious one. Later, however, he accepts this doctrine as meaning that evil cannot be radically bad, since it acts as a necessary antecedent condition of good. Evil makes necessary the struggle for the good which is "the chief value of life in this world." The Gospels imply a religious monism combined with an ethical dualism which, while theoretically inconsistent, is a solution that "works." Finally, Christian Platonism has correctly analyzed moral evil as rooted in finite creatures' proud self-love.[60]

Inge's doctrine of salvation is based upon a diagnosis of Western culture which concludes that we have come to a genuine *fin de siècle*. After the First World War Inge refused to predict a renaissance of the human spirit. But after the Second World War he flatly predicted a "revival of spiritual and unworldly religion" in England and Europe, basing this upon the tendency of human nature to seek compensations. The major objection to the Christian Platonist view of salvation is that it is "escapism." Inge's reply to this is a *tu quoque*: so are all other forms of salvation, whether archaism, futurism, or acosmism. The flight of the Christian Platonist is vindicated if it is true that the spiritual world is the real world, and that social troubles result from false standards of values. The permanent value of Christian Platonism lies in its conviction that we look in vain to the *kosmos aisthetos* for solutions to our problems which arise from our ignorance of the *kosmos noetos*.

*Critical Remarks and Conclusion.* Inge's conception of the relation of Neo-Platonism and Christianity is not sufficiently critical. In both, Love and "assimilation to God" play important roles. But Plato's *Eros*, although called a god, is essentially man's urge toward the vision of the ideal; and Plotinus' *nous eron* is very similar to Spinoza's *amor intellectualis dei*. Although it may be overstressed, there is a difference between the classical *Eros* and the Christian *Agape*. One enables man to do what he ought to do for himself; the other does for man what he cannot do for himself. It is no service to either Christianity or Platonism to neglect the fact that the one is essentially theocentric, while the other is anthropocentric and cosmocentric.

Inge has an inconsistent view of the relation of man and Nature. Generally he holds that Nature is all-inclusive, including "the divine life on earth of Jesus Christ." Elsewhere he speaks of man's ideals and self-determination as unique, without analogy to the rest of creation.[61] Indecisiveness as a characteristic feature of Inge's mind is strikingly revealed in his opinions on Wordsworth's Platonism. In *Studies of English Mystics* (1906) he calls Wordsworth more Stoic than Platonic because it is the sense of eternal and ubiquitous life, and not of the beauty of Nature, which is central in his thought. In *The Platonic Tradition in English Religious Thought* (1926) he reverses this opinion and calls Wordsworth not only one to whom Platonism came naturally, but a Platonic panentheist in doctrine. Finally, in *Mysticism in Religion* (1947) he reverts to his former opinion and finds Wordsworth's place as a nature-mystic taken by Traherne. Inge's inconclusiveness indicates that he did not have a clear conception of what he meant by Platonism over the course of his writings.

Inge's doctrine of religious knowledge is weak. He continually talks of "Reason" but relies upon an undefined form of intuition. His so-called ontological proof of the existence of God bears little relation to Anselm's thought, since it is simply an expansion of the Thomistic dictum "impossible est naturale desiderium esse inane."[62] His conception of the nature and function of religious symbols is superficial because it does not face up to the central problem of the nature and existence of what is symbolized. Inge is logically committed to a sacramental view of Nature, but he actually makes very little use of the concept. He is so impressed with the Law of Entropy for the apparent support which it gives to his doctrine of the eternal world that he is blind to the philosophical contributions of biologically oriented thought. This results in a misrepresentation of Christian Platonism, as the thought of Taylor and Temple shows.

Inge is inconsistent on the point whether values are the revealed attributes of God or whether they make up a spiritual world which is metaphysically prior to God. He gives superficial treatment to the problem of the "objective existence" of values, being content to assert that they must be real. Actually, he has two different conceptions of values, as human ideals and as cosmic existents, and he does not reconcile them. If values energize themselves there is no need to introduce into the universe man's "purposive production of values." But if it is man alone who "introduces final causes into the processes of nature," there is no reason why values should be regarded as objective existences, except after they are realized.[63] Inge's conception of the relation of fact and value is confused. Thus, on the one hand he holds that Höffding's phrase "the conservation of values" is inapplicable to what is timeless because it is a metaphor drawn from the time-series, while on the other hand he says that the phrase is identical in meaning with Plotinus' *apoletai ouden ton onton.* Finally, in direct contradiction to the Platonic axiom that what is most real ought to be best known, Inge joins the *philopseudeis* and holds that because of our necessary ignorance about ultimate matters we must turn to myth for illumination.[64]

Inge mentions that a "sacramental view of history" may be held on Christian Platonist grounds, but he does not develop this important conception. He is unwilling to allow to certain historical persons and events the ultimate significance which Christianity ascribes to them, thinking that it would disturb his Platonism. If he were more conversant with the *Timaeus,* he would see that there is a place in Platonism for a historical view of temporal reality, as Taylor and Whitehead point out.

Inge ranks as a minor figure in Christian Platonism. He is neither an original nor a reliable interpreter of that tradition. His attempt to construct an amalgam of Christian Platonism is unsuccessful because he does not clearly and deeply analyze the essential ideas of either Christianity or Platonism. Because of his lack of high philosophical competence, and his inability to produce a clear, critical conception of Christian Platonism as a whole, he cannot bring that tradition to bear with much force upon contemporary man's religious problems.

# II: The Christian Platonism
## of Paul Elmer More

PAUL ELMER MORE (1864–1937), the only American-born Platonist whom we are considering, led a literary and academic career. After graduate studies at Harvard (1892–1900) he became literary editor of the *Independent* in 1901. From 1903–9 he held the same position with the New York *Evening Post*. In 1909 he became editor of the *Nation*, held this post until 1914, and continued as advisory editor for some years thereafter. He continually advocated the application of ethical criteria to contemporary literature. In this, and as a leader among the "American Humanists," he was closely associated with Irving Babbitt in opposing Romanticism and Modernism. These themes are apparent in the many essays which he wrote, most of which are collected in his eleven-volume *Shelburne Essays*. As a lecturer, first in philosophy and later in classics at Princeton University (1918-32), he produced his major work, the six-volume *The Greek Tradition*, which covers the period from the death of Socrates to the Council of Chalcedon. Upon his conversion to Anglo-Catholic Christianity (he was never confirmed) he gave the Lowell Lectures, which are embodied in *The Sceptical Approach to Religion*. Just before he died he completed his *apologia pro vita sua*, *Pages from an Oxford Diary*.

More reacted violently from the Calvinism of his home, and successively embraced German Romanticism, Rationalism, and Materialism. Before he returned to Christianity the central concept in his thought—"dualism"—was fixed.

His dualism was confirmed by his studies of Indian religious thought, Manichaeism, and Platonism. He contends that a moral dualism—a clear consciousness of a cleavage in human nature between good and evil tendencies—is the basis of all highly developed religions. Where philosophy would explain it away and where literature would imaginatively dissolve it, religion accepts the fact of dualism, holding also that the gulf may be bridged by "self-surrender to a power . . . not ourselves."[1]

*The Religious Thought of Socrates and Plato.* The thesis of *The Greek Tradition* is that the genuine elements which comprise Christian Platonism form a harmonious whole, and that there are several alien intrusions which must be rejected.[2] The distortion of Christian Platonism which has prevailed since the Council of Chalcedon was that reactionary and barbarian form which was begun in Alexandria by the Neo-Platonists, and which was carried on by the Latins and Teutons. Without genuine Platonism the West would have lapsed into barbarism altogether, and is in danger of doing so today unless it is recovered. With Cicero, More regards those dissident to Platonism as *plebeii philosophi.* Historically, Platonism has been ambivalent. In pseudo-Platonism *mousikos eran* leads to the "vagaries of minds drunk with the excess of enthusiasm." In genuine Platonism there is always a correlative factor of equal and opposite force, a criterion of impulses which was historically rooted in the religion of the Platonic Socrates. This More calls the "inner check" or (following Babbitt) the *frein vital,* which is the exact antithesis of Bergson's romantic *élan vital.*

More holds that Plato, in the biographical portions of the *Apology, Crito,* and *Phaedo,* presents a reasonably faithful portrait of the historical Socrates as well as the basic origin of his own thought. The *Gorgias* indicates the point where Plato stops thinking Socrates' thought after him, and begins to bring his own thought to mature expression. In 1917 More held that the Socratic germ plasm of Platonism consisted of three elements: "an intellectual scepticism, a spiritual affirmation, and a tenacious belief in the identity of virtue and knowledge." In 1934 he adds the conception of a genuine teleology, holding that Socrates' critique of Anaxagoras' doctrine of *Nous* (*Phaedo* 96 ff.) is "the most important and significant and revolutionary event in the whole range of philosophy."[3] Socrates rejected the immanent, mechanical conception of *telos* and pointed toward the conception which Plato was to develop into ethical Theism. Socrates' scepticism was not an Academic absolute suspension of judgment but a process of radical doubt which cleared the ground for a solidly founded moral philosophy. This form of scepticism is not incompatible with "spiritual affirmation" which More describes as insight consisting of the "supra-rational intuition" of the inner check and the infra-rational intuition of the flux of impulses. Socrates did not try to make these two elements cohere with one another, nor with the equation of virtue and knowledge. This task was left to Plato, and we must accept the paradoxical character of Socrates as a "rationalizing utilitarian and a sceptical mystic."

What More calls "the Religion of Plato" includes three basic components. Philosophy discusses the paradox of the identity of virtue and knowledge. Theology is the rationale of the divine. Mythology is discourse about the intermingling of the human and the divine, as well as the poetic expression of truths which cannot be rationally explained. As a parallel movement to the course of Plato's thought as represented in this threefold scheme, there is also his harmonious development of the Socratic theses. In the course of his thought More changes his mind as to how the integration took place. Earlier he contended that in the *Republic* (which he regarded as an organic unity) Plato harmonized

the Socratic theses in the Idea of the Good, which was the
consummate expression of his religious thought. Later, while
More's formulation of Plato's conclusion does not change
("Man is intellectually impotent and morally responsible"),
he finds that Plato confuses philosophy and religion in the
Euthyphro, absolutely separates them in the Republic, and
regards them as parallel and mutually confirmatory in the
Timaeus and Laws.[4]

More interprets the body-soul dualism of Plato morally
rather than metaphysically, as showing that "the distinctive
mark of man is a consciously directive will." Man's summum
bonum is eudaimonia, which is to be distinguished from
hedone, and defined as "a measured harmony and the unity
of subordination." From the fundamental dualism of happiness and pleasure Plato's other dualisms arose. Thus, the
dualism of knowledge and opinion arises from the cleft between supra-rational and infra-rational intuition. Similarly,
Plato's psychology is not a rigid tripartitism but a dualism
of the higher and lower parts of the soul. In relation to to
thymoeides and to epithymetikon, nous is the governing
element of the soul. It should not be confused with the
liberum arbitrium, but in Plato's thought functions discur-
sively, intuitively, and ethically (as the daimonion enan-
tioma of Alcibiades 103a). By the inner check man knows
that his misery and happiness are within his own jurisdic-
tion; yet he also knows that much of his pleasure and pain
is not—a fact which implies determinism and irresponsi-
bility. It was Plato's recognition of the "irreconcilable paradox" arising from the facts of human freedom and irrespon-
sibility that brought him to say, "To every man his all is
dual" (Laws 726), and provided the stimulus for his development of the doctrine of Ideas.[5]

More finds two main classes of Ideas in the dialogues—
the rational and the ethical—and says that to confuse them
is a "disastrous misunderstanding" of Plato's method. The

first class consists of mathematical forms and intellectual generalizations, both of which have a "pragmatical reality." The difference between the two classes of Ideas lies in the way in which the members of each are known: moral Ideas by the intuitive possession of philosophical insight, and rational Ideas by the discursive methods of scientific inquiry. Moral Ideas are objective realities existing apart from our knowledge of them, and at the same time they are "imaginative projections of the facts of our moral consciousness." Although Plato did not satisfactorily explain how particulars participate in universals, he avoided the rationalistic and romantic errors in their interpretation. Plotinus succumbed to both, while Santayana exemplifies the latter. Instead of creating Ideas *ex nihilo*, the imagination gives vitality and pertinence to the moral facts disclosed to the religious consciousness.[6]

Fundamentally, More interprets Ideas in terms of what Inge (following Stewart) calls "visualism," calling attention to *Symposium* 219a and *Republic* 475e. The ontological status of Ideas depends, in part, upon the degree of intensity with which they are regarded. Considered academically, they are implausible; vitally appropriated, they are objectively authoritative for feeling and conduct. But More differs from Inge in holding that the demonstration of the truth of Ideas partly depends upon the consequences of believing in them. In his final position, More is more definite than Inge in holding that the Idea of the Good is not Plato's surrogate for God. In the *Timaeus*, there are three causes— the Ideas, the Demiurge, and the matrix—hence the Idea of the Good is not the Absolute. Finally, more weight should be given to the theological and mythological components of Plato's religion. Scepticism and spiritual affirmation are exhausted in the conception of Ideas. The Socratic identification of virtue and knowledge cannot be demonstrated by philosophy. The theory of Ideas, while it combines the moral and the otherworldly aspects of religion, fails of religious adequacy because it tends to neglect the concept of personality.

While Plato held that rational and ethical Ideas were eternal realities, in his later thought he wandered into an enigmatic mathematicism in which scientific interests ousted the ethical dialectic. The Neo-Realist reduction of Ideas to mathematical entities is unjustified, because Plato's mathematical interest (in the One and the Many) was an abstraction from his underlying ethical dualism. However, Plato's thought was never "metaphysical," by which More means an uncritical, monistic rationalism.[7] The *Parmenides* and the *Sophist* show that Plato finally held that the Ideas were not reached as the conclusion of a process of discursive thought, but were known in "some direct experience" independent of logic.

Plato's theory of Ideas is valuable today in refuting both metaphysical absolutism and pragmatism. William James and John Dewey reject the critical function of reason, and deny its "supra-rational intuition of the absolute," although they agree with Plato's analysis of the flux and contingency of the temporal world.[8] Whitehead's rationalism is both deistic and antihumanistic. The "principle of concretion" is ultimately an impersonal principle, and his "organic mechanism" ignores the fact that "a stone and the human soul cannot be brought under the same definition."[9]

The religion of Plato is an integral part of the Greek Tradition, arising from the thought of Socrates and pointing forward to Christianity. The transition from Socraticism to the development of his own thought begins when Plato realizes that philosophy is unable to establish the identity of virtue and knowledge. Since merit and reward are frequently disparate in this world, the failure comes to the same thing as inability to prove the immortality of the soul. Plato never held a doctrine of impersonal immortality,

although in the *Republic* as a *tour de force* he attempted
to establish the superiority of justice over injustice on the
basis of pure philosophy alone. In the theistically oriented
*Timaeus* and *Laws*, then, we see the essence of Plato's religious thought.[10]

By Plato's theology More means "the science of God,
the consideration of His nature in itself," and, like Taylor,
selects *Laws* X as the basis of his study. Plato sought to
establish the existence of God(s) by three methods: from
design, from the *consensus gentium*, and from the nature
of the soul in man and the world. His formal teleological
proof is not logically coercive, but it is superior to mechanistic materialism, overweening rationalism, and atheism and
agnosticism. All the efforts of pure reason to establish the
existence of an absolute and infinite Being fail because they
presume a knowledge of ultimate principles which man does
not have. As Plato shows, according to *hoi tupoi peri the-
ologias* (*Republic* 379a) our actual knowledge leads to a
God finite in all attributes but goodness. Hence a true
theism must be based upon Plato's "inference from design,
refurbished in the light of modern science." Its essential
elements are found in the conception of Purpose as cosmic
in extent, although thwarted by "obstacles and difficulties."[11] Nevertheless, Plato's strongest evidence for the
existence of God is derived from the "soul's own consciousness of itself," and his theology is really an ethical
sequel to Socrates' conviction that it is better to do justice
and suffer injustice than to do injustice, although man may
be ignorant of all else.

More's final argument against the identification of God
and the Idea of the Good is based on an analysis of teleology
in which the *Republic* and the *Timaeus* are taken as sup-
plementary. The Idea of the Good is the final cause of the
universe, while the Demiurge is its primary efficient cause.
He also holds that there are three other major misinterpre-

tations of Plato's theology. Plato is not a deist, because the Demiurge is pictured in terms of personality. He is not a pantheist, because he distinguished between the Demiurge and the "World Soul." He is not a Manichaean, because the evil world soul suggested in *Laws* 896e plays no important role in his thought.[12]

Like Inge, More regards Plato's mythology as containing his dramatic solutions to the problems of cosmogony and theodicy. Its *locus classicus* is the *Timaeus*, which More calls an "allegory of our inner experience" and the consummation of Plato's religious thought. Plato was driven to mythology because that was the only way to elaborate the cosmic dualism corresponding to the dualism of man's moral experience. Since the doctrine of *methexis* failed to explain how *noumena* and *phainomena* can be distinguished yet interrelated, Plato ultimately solved the problem by making God "the dynamic element in Ideas." Although there is a superficial dualism in the *Timaeus* between *to on aei* and *to gignomenon*, Plato's main purpose was not cosmological, but was to elucidate the "fact of consciousness that in our one person two contrary and irreconciliable natures co-exist." Plato's *hupodoche* or "necessary cause" is not to be identified with evil as the necessary condition of the good, but refers to "something intrinsically evil." Although Plato has no metaphysical solution to the problem of evil, he finally identifies evil with the Socratic *amathia*, an ignorance of the self which is nourished by self-love.[13]

As a consequence of harmonizing the Socratic theses, Plato showed that religion connects both philosophy and theology. The aim of philosophy is to make righteousness the end of life, which, religiously interpreted, means paying honor to the divine soul. Again, the "mythological notion of measure" is religion's way of making religious thought practical. Since justice is unstable, our knowledge of it is never final. This affords a difficulty for man, since morality obliges him to be just. Consequently, the only way he can be just is to be mythologically related to "God the measure of all things," and thus be a participant in the redemptive, cosmic drama.[14]

*Critical Remarks on More's Conception of Platonism.* More's denial of the continuity of the Platonic tradition is without historical foundation, as the studies of Muirhead and Lovejoy clearly show. By finding the culmination of Platonism in the formula of Chalcedon, and by regarding Neo-Platonism as a heresy, he creates an artificial gap of 1,500 years, with the untenable implication that genuine Platonism lay dormant or contaminated until he revived and cleansed it. More's use of the "inner check" as the criterion between true and false Platonism is an oversimplification. Even Taylor, who stresses the religious quality of Socrates' thought and life, is unable to say how seriously the *daimonion* should be taken. More develops this criterion in order to exclude what he regards as the immoral romanticism of Plotinus from Platonism, failing to recognize that Plotinus was a sober moralist in the classical tradition, as well as a God-seeking mystic.

While More recognizes the significance of Socrates, he does not present a satisfactory conception of his relation to Plato. His treatment of Plato's development of the Socratic theses introduces an artificial schematism which the dialogues do not support. Plato never held that philosophy and religion were combined by regarding the Idea of the Good as God. Nor did he ever hold that philosophy and religion were unrelated. What he does hold in the *Euthyphro*, the *Republic*, and the *Laws* is that traditional religious notions and practices must be judged by a rational, comprehensive moral philosophy.

It is highly gratuitous to attribute the origin of Plato's ontological and epistemological dualism to a subjective moral dualism. Not only is More's analysis of the dialogues uncritical, but he erroneously regards all of the *Epistles* as "forgeries," and rejects Plato's oral teaching in the Academy. This unwarranted obscurantism exaggerates his already one-sidedly moralistic interpretation of Plato's Ideas. As Taylor and Whitehead point out, in the Academy Plato regarded Forms as Numbers—a justifiable position since both mathematics and ethics are concerned with ideal, abstract patterns. More is thoroughly confused in his analysis of such Ideas as Justice. On the one hand, he correctly points out that Plato regarded them as normatively real, and not simply concepts in the human mind. On the other hand, he offers a psychological interpretation of Ideas as "imaginative projections" of moral facts. There is no warrant whatsoever for such a subjective interpretation in Plato. In an isolated passage[15] More discusses the possibility that *nous* and *noeta* may affect each other reciprocally, that Ideas are objectively real but that the human mind plays a creative role in their apprehension, thus approaching Inge's view.

More gives no reason for choosing between the various characterizations of Ideas which he presents, and fails to show how they may be reconciled. He describes them as (1) "an emphatic assertion of the unchanging reality behind moral forces," (2) "imaginative projections of the facts of moral consciousness," and (3) "the immediate vision of moral forces as ideal entities."[16] Beside being unreconciled (1) and (2) have no warrant in Plato. (3) is closer to the truth, but More ignores the fact that in the *Republic* long and rigorous intellectual training must be undergone before there is a vision of the Idea of the Good, and that it is of the Good as such, and not of a moral force as an ideal entity.

There is no evidence for More's thesis that Plato despaired of finding philosophical answers to religious questions and so resorted to theology and mythology. His sharp distinction between these three forms of thought is without foundation, since Plato combined all three as early as the *Republic* and as late as the *Timaeus*. More's view involves him in the awkward and fanciful conjecture that Plato voluntarily suspended his firm conviction in personal immortality in the *Republic* in order rationally to prove that justice was better than injustice.

More's polemic discussions of "metaphysics" clearly reveal his bias in philosophy. He does not see that Plato's "dialectic" was metaphysics in so far as it consisted of critical analysis of fundamental concepts, for the sake of understanding them in themselves, and as a whole in their relation to reality. More has no recognition whatever of the Platonic elements in Whitehead's thought. Furthermore, Whitehead does not try to bring a stone and the human soul "under the same definition" (whatever that may mean), but attempts to show their structural and dynamic similarities. One of the few merits of More's rigidly dualistic interpretation of Plato is that it has more foundation than Inge's totally uncritical statement, "There is no sense in which dualism can be attributed to Plato."[17]

More is correct in pointing out that Plato's Demiurge was a finite deity, but wrong in his reasons. As Inge and Taylor show, compared to Plotinus' One Plato's Demiurge is finite because the *paradeigma* are metaphysically prior to it. Matter is not the intractable cause of the imperfection of the world. Plato does not stress the obstructive qualities of Becoming and the matrix, but their susceptibility to persuasion by *nous*. The reason the world is not perfect is due to Plato's doctrine of causality, which holds that the effect mirrors the cause.[18] More inconsistently holds that Plato's theology is more reasonable than its alternatives, but that even it is "fundamentally irrational."[19] More anachronistically attributes "personality" to Plato's God, and

totally ignores the question whether this concept is to be
applied to God univocally or analogically. He does not explore the fact that Plato held a doctrine of God *and* the
World Soul, and that some form of divine immanence in
the world has always been an element of the Platonic tradition. His mythological interpretation of the *Timaeus* is inadequate, to say the least. He makes the jejune statement
that the discussion of Time and Eternity there merely
registers Plato's awareness of the distinction between the
mutable and the immutable.[20] There is no ground whatever for making the Demiurge "the dynamic element" of
Ideas. Both have *dunamis*, but they are not identified on
this or any other basis.

In conclusion, we can find no reason for agreeing with
Robin that More's study of Plato has a "valeur originale et
puissante." As an expositor and interpreter of the religious
thought of Plato, More is thoroughly unreliable. He ob-
trudes his own preconceptions upon Plato not to illuminate
him, but to distort him almost beyond recognition. To interpret Plato exclusively in terms of a moralistic and obscurantistic dualism has nothing to recommend it except its
quality of being an ingenious *tour de force*.

*Platonism and Christianity and Their Perversions.* From
Platonism as a *preparatio evangelica* to *Christus Consum-
mator* is the formula which expresses the course of More's
constructive thought. What Plato's dialogues prefigure,
the Christ of the New Testament and of Greek *Logos-*
theology perfects. Socratic *autarkeia* and *apatheia* are not
negated, but perfected, by the disclosure of God in the
Incarnation. The integration of Platonism and Christianity
is historically justifiable, as against Harnack's depreciation
of the Hellenization of Christianity. Clement of Alexandria
illustrates the truth that, while Christianity originated in
Palestine, it spread only when translated into the more

universal terms of Greek thought. Furthermore, the components of Plato's religion indicate the basic structure of Christianity, despite the fact that they are differently evaluated. Where Plato began with philosophy and proceeded with lessening assurance through theology and mythology, Christianity reversed the process. It began with a myth, regarded as a "demonstrable event of history" and as the criterion of its subsequent religious thought.

Similarities between Platonism and Christianity can be seen in the doctrine of the imitation of God and in their attitude towards the "distinctive reality and importance of the soul."[21] Again, Platonism sometimes provides the foundation for the Christian superstructure, and at the same time purifies it of alien intrusions. Thus, St. Paul combines Platonic ethical and metaphysical dualism with his Hebraic eschatological faith, an unstable compound of which Platonism is the valuable ingredient.[22]

The dogma of the Incarnation is not a metaphysical theory, but a "conviction born of experience." Although historically unique, it was not an isolated event, but the *peripeteia* of history. It is so important that "religion itself" is at stake in our acceptance or rejection of it.[23] Christ as *a* man made palpable and prophetic Plato's poetic adumbrations of the Ideas. And in Greek theology's doctrine of the eternal Christ Plato's problem of "participation" was solved: the Ideas were personified in the divine Logos, while as impersonal laws of beauty and justice they were nevertheless entities in their own right. The doctrine of Christ as God and *man*, as formulated in the Definition of Chalcedon (451), at once preserves the original and essential truth of Christianity and fulfills the Platonic dualism. It limited baseless speculations, and was consistent with man's deepest spiritual experience. It stated with finality what Plato anticipated when he saw that man had two "utterly disparate natures" although he lived in one world.[24]

The revelational character of the Logos completes Platonism mythologically and teleologically. The religious quest
cannot rest in the poetic embodiments of reasonable con-
jectures, but demands the certainty of revelation in which
God descends to man and man arises to God. The Logos
reveals itself progressively through the strata of creation,
culminating in man conscious of himself as a purposive
agent who can not only infer the existence of purpose in
the inanimate and animate worlds but can "communicate
his self-knowledge to other men." This inescapable inference of the Platonist and the great theistic world-religions
is confirmed by the Incarnation in which the divine love
achieves its purpose only through self-surrender and voluntary suffering.[25]

More's conception of the mutually supporting, clarify-
ing, and purifying relations between Platonism and Christianity is clearly shown in his discussion of the Eucharist.
The sacramental idea rests upon a dualistic conception of
the world in which matter and spirit are "essentially distinct
yet mutually interdependent." The Platonic Ideas are not
regarded as mere symbols, but as morally authoritative
realities. Plato's conception of the total activity of the good
creator in the *Timaeus* provides a foundation for the sacramental idea which is both spiritual and realistic. But while
Plato (and his disciples and critics) was perplexed with the
problem of "participation," Christianity solved it in its
doctrine that the sacramental change "represents (*reprae-
sentat, paristesi,* in the sense of making actually present)"
the divine drama of redemption. This expression of the
sacramental idea in Patristic Christian Platonism is far
superior to subsequent materializations and attenuations because it combines both Platonism and Christianity at their
best.[26]

Neo-Platonism is an almost complete perversion of the
religious thought of Plato. While a useful protest against

Epicurean and Stoic materialism, the *Enneads* either explained away evil or sought to evade it by an amoral doctrine of salvation. In the final absorptive state, the theistic doctrine of man's communion with God is irrelevant and the essential dualistic structure of religious thought is dissolved in an excessive rationalism and *Mysticismus*. Neo-Platonism is basically more Aristotelian than Platonic. Aristotle's "Unmoved Mover" creates a radical disjunction between God and the world, and thus provides a basis for Plotinus' absolute mysticism. Furthermore, Aristotle's denial that Plato's Ideas were "separate" from particulars removed a barrier to Plotinus' mystical appropriation of Ideas. It is Plotinus' doctrine of the ultimate coalescence of knower and known which absolutely distinguishes Neo-Platonism from Platonism.

Much of Plotinus' thought consists of transforming his personal experience into a "cosmic mythology" which is congenial with Platonism. But Plotinus metaphysically distorted his psychological analysis of *nous* and hypostatized it as the absolute, abstract unity from which all being mechanically emanates. Where Plato made *Ananke* contrary to the Good, Plotinus made it inherent in the Good, and the consequence was a specious rationalistic optimism which is religiously stultifying. Plotinus' romantic abuse of the imagination corresponds to his abuse of reason. Both arise through ignoring the Socratic inner check, going beyond the Platonic dualism, and interpreting the Ideas subjectively. The final religious inadequacy of Plotinus is his doctrine of absorptive mysticism. He gave "spiritual catalepsy" an evidential value it does not possess, and transmuted a state of complete ignorance into unqualified knowledge. In rebellion against the truth that "we are morally responsible and intellectually impotent," his mysticism culminates with "the most terrible word in our Western philosophy"—" 'the flight of the alone to the Alone.' "[27]

There are three major forms of mysticism represented in Platonism and Christianity. The first is founded upon the dualism between supernatural realities and an illusory phenomenal world, and is perfectly congenial with Christian Platonism. The second form, while it tends to dissolve the dualism of the first, can be reconciled with Christian Platonism, as the *Theological Orations* of Gregory Nazianzen show. The third form is the absorptive variety of which Plotinus is the prototype in the Western world and which is represented in Augustine. This form is not really congenial with Christianity because it has no place for the doctrine of the Incarnation and the sacramental view of the universe, and dehumanizes man as well as depersonalizes God.[28]

More concludes the final volume of his *Greek Tradition* with a plea for the restriction of Christian religious thought within the limits of traditional orthodoxy and Platonic Idealism. Two major problems of a contemporary version of this type of thought concern the nature of Faith and Hope. In dealing with the former More insists that religion is not an exercise in pious self-delusion. Christian Platonism will not tolerate the substitution of what we might like to be true for what we actually believe to be true. Faith is a kind of "inferential knowledge" midway between Plato's *episteme* and the modern pragmatist's "will to believe." In its knowledge of the "immediate affections" of the moral sense it is comparable to the Aristotelian *aisthesis*. Since man also gains knowledge of the external world through observation, the paradox results that to his intuition he is conscious of freedom and responsibility, while to observation he seems mechanically determined. By faith man projects his immediate sense of personal freedom into the world at large. The whole world then becomes teleological, and "religion is an attempt to live in harmony with a world so conceived." While this conception of faith is admittedly anthropomorphic, it is not wishful thinking, because religious faith consists of "an unremitting determination to transmute a probability of belief into a truth of experience."[29]

Contemporary man is obliged to choose between two alternatives: the hopelessness of Prometheus on his rock, and the hopefulness which Christian Platonism inspires. The sceptic sees that reason is impotent to decide between these alternatives. Consequently, religious knowledge is neither rationalistic or fideistic, but "a certainty of being in the right way, a pragmatic assurance that faith is pointing towards reality, a gift of divine hope."[30]

*Critical Remarks and Conclusion.* Most of the parallels which More draws between Platonism and Christianity are superficial and obvious. Of what value is it to compare the allegory of the *Phaedrus* with the eighth chapter of John and say that Jesus' fulfillment of the Platonic vision is "the greatest moment in the history of human thought"?[31] No historical connection is shown; no rational connections are explained. Again, if Platonism is the foundation of Greek theology and the Demiurge is the essence of Plato's theology, why does not More show that Plato's finite God was highly influential in Greek theology? He does not because he cannot. Plato's Demiurge has been historically and intellectually negligible, except among the Gnostics. Certainly Christian orthodoxy has considered it negligible as compared to Plotinus' One. Again, there is no historical evidence that the Definition of Chalcedon is the culmination of Plato's dualistic theism. It is simply a notion which rounds off More's highly schematic thesis. Furthermore, even to hold this position More has to soften the "unabsolved dualism" which he so strenuously advocated by asserting some rational connection between matter and spirit.

A self-styled defender of Christian orthodoxy, More nevertheless indulges in the peculiar heresy of "Binitarianism." The doctrine of the Trinity is rejected and "some indefinable dualism" is introduced into the Godhead, so that God may manifest Himself in the Incarnation and yet remain essentially intact. This notion has neither religious value nor philosophical depth to commend it. His conception of Matter as the evil Necessity which resists divine purpose is a quasi-Manichaean notion which has no support in orthodox Christian thought. More is no better an expositor of Christianity than he is of Platonism, and for the same reason: he brings to his subject neither the erudition nor the originality required.

More's uncritical hostility toward Plotinus more than matches Inge's uncritical adulation. Typical of the loose vituperation which characterizes his presentation of Plotinus is the assertion that the "most deplorable event in the history of philosophy" occurred when Neo-Platonism "swallowed up" Platonism.[32] There is no evidence that this happened. The real issue between Inge and More is whether the *Enneads* are a legitimate development or an illicit perversion of Plato's dialogues. While More is more clearly aware than Inge of the differences between Platonism and Neo-Platonism, they are not as radical as he supposes. The most striking instance of More's distortion of Plotinus is his insistence that the essence of his religious thought rests upon the peripheral experience of *ekstasis*. Porphyry says that this happened only four times to Plotinus, and it is clearly absurd to make his metaphysics rest solely upon the " 'flight of the alone to the Alone' " and dismiss his essentially classical world-view as a crude mixture of romantic fancy and baseless speculation. It is unhistorical for More to regard Aristotle as the sole source of Plotinus' transcendentalism and unitive theory of knowledge since the seeds of both are found in the *Republic*.[33] It is an over-

simplification of Plotinus' thought to say that he makes
*Ananke* inherent in the Good since, as Inge points out,
Plotinus also regards it as resisting the Good.

More's interpretation of Plotinus is less judicious than
Inge's. There is no sound reason for dividing the person
of Plotinus into a "saint" and a "metaphysician," as if it
were impossible for the same man to be both at once. After
all, Plotinus actually sought to formulate a system of philosophical thought, in many instances profoundly religious,
which would delineate a total way of life for the whole
man in a generously conceived world. To construe Plotinus' mysticism primarily in terms of "absorption" and "an-
nihilation" ignores the role of Ideas which constitutes one
of its genuinely Platonic elements. It is not a sound interpretation of either Plato or Plotinus which leads More to
cast upon Neo-Platonism, as Robin puts it, "un anathème
impitoyable."

More's division of mysticism into three planes is another
illustration of the artificially schematic form of his thought.
There is more historical foundation for Inge's distinction
between introspective and speculative mysticism. However,
More is correct in pointing out that mysticism is not altogether congenial with the orthodox Christian doctrine of
the Incarnation. Inge, for example, fails to integrate that
doctrine with Neo-Platonic mysticism, and his treatment of
the sacramental idea is weak. But if mysticism be defined
as emotionally intense and rationally scrupulous communion with God, and sacramentalism as the spiritual use
of natural things, then both St. John and St. Paul show
how the classical Christian faith combines them both. It is
only because of his superficial, arbitrary, and inaccurate
treatment of mysticism that More is able to conclude that it
is a "disease of religion" and "the handiwork of the Demon
of the Absolute."[34]

More correctly insists with Inge that Christianity must

be accepted on the basis of its "objective truth" rather than upon its appeal to imagination or will. Inge's thought does not satisfy this ideal because he arbitrarily restricts the range of admissible evidence to inner experience. More is even further from satisfying it because he insists that man is "intellectually incompetent." His doctrine of faith seems to be a concession to the fashionable anthropomorphic interpretation of religion. In the Judaeo-Christian tradition faith is elicited by God's disclosure of Himself in the Covenant or the Incarnation. More's thoroughly obscurantistic view of human reason prevents him from understanding the nature of theistic proof. Taylor, for example, does not hold that the existence of God can be demonstrated. But given faith in God, reason can show that it is no less rationally grounded, and perhaps more so, than nontheistic alternatives.[35]

The tradition of Christian Platonism which was so well served by Clement, Origen, Augustine, and Bonaventura is meagerly represented by Inge and More. Both cannot be Christian Platonists, if the term is to retain any distinctive meaning, since they are in contradiction on many important points. Inge is closer to the Platonic tradition as that has historically developed. Muirhead points out that Platonism is primarily concerned with the problem of the relation of value and existence, and holds that all other facts must be interpreted in the light of the fact of value. Inge recognizes this truth, but his treatment of the subject is superficial; while More's dualism amounts to an aggravation of the problem.

Muirhead lists as the doctrines which make up the vital structure of Platonism the following: (1) the distinction between appearance and reality, (2) that the separateness of things is phenomenal, while the differences between things are real, (3) that the order of reality is essentially teleological, and (4) that this order appears in man as conscious purpose.[36] It is clear that Inge's cosmocentric Idealism is closer to the first two doctrines, while More's anthropocentrism and finite theism is closer to the last two doctrines. On this basis each is half a Platonist, but we cannot get a complete Platonist by synthesizing their positions. However, superficial verbal opposition between the two men should not blind us to their underlying similarities of meaning. Thus, More must soften his strict dualism between matter and spirit in order to give an intelligible account of the sacraments; and there is no substantial difference between their theories of religious knowledge since both ultimately rely on intuition, whether it be called "mystical" or "supra-rational."

Inge and More reflect within their own thought significant differences within the Platonic tradition. Inge adopts Plotinus' fluid conception of the soul, and More adopts Socrates' and Plato's conception of the soul as the seat of moral personality. Inge adopts Plotinus' absolute One, while More adopts Plato's finite deity. Inge regards the Platonic conceptions as immature, and More regards Plotinus' conceptions as excrescences upon Platonism. Both views tend to fragmentize the Platonic tradition which historically includes the thought of both Plato and Plotinus. Both Inge and More are weak in dealing with the concept of Nature, as understood in the Platonic tradition. Inge despises the sensible and temporal world because he is preoccupied with an invisible realm of eternal values. More is unable to penetrate beneath the surface of fluent reality because his dualism is too rigid to permit it.

Both would integrate Platonism and Christianity to the maximum degree, but they fail to do justice to either, and produce a concoction rather than an amalgam. Inge distorts Christianity because he depreciates its integral Hebraic heritage and its fundamental dependence upon historical persons and events. More distorts Christianity because his thought is essentially moralistic, dualistic, and obscurantist. Along with their weaknesses of historical interpretation and systematic thought, they fail to show that Christian Platonism is really relevant to contemporary religious problems. Acosmism and pietism have nothing to do with either Platonism or Christianity at its best. Derivative and arbitrary presentations of Christian Platonism do not advance that tradition. What is needed if today this tradition is to reflect its past dignity and appeal to thoughtful religious persons is a more thorough and profound understanding of the philosophical depth of Platonism and of the religious genius of Christianity, and an ability to grapple with fundamental problems.

# III: The Christian Platonism
of A. E. Taylor

THE SON of a Wesleyan minister, Alfred Edward Taylor
was born at Oundle on December 22, 1869, and died in
his sleep at Edinburgh on October 31, 1945. He was educated at Kingswood School, Bath, and at New College,
Oxford. As a Fellow of Merton College he began an intimate and lifelong friendship with F. H. Bradley whose
influence largely dominated his early thought, as can be
seen in *The Problem of Conduct* (1901) and *Elements of
Metaphysics* (1903). In 1896 Samuel Alexander secured
Taylor's services as Lecturer in Greek and Philosophy at
Owen's College, Manchester. Taylor remained there until
1903 and under Alexander's influence reacted from Absolute Idealism "towards the empirical and given."[1] From
1903 until 1908 Taylor was Professor of Philosophy at Mc-
Gill University, Montreal. In 1908 he succeeded Bosanquet
as Professor of Moral Philosophy at St.Andrew's. He remained there until 1924 when he was called to the Chair of
Moral Philosophy at Edinburgh, a post which he held until
his retirement in 1941.

Most aspects of Taylor's wide erudition converge in his
studies of Platonism which, throughout his writings, he
sought to relate to his other current interests. The essence of
his religious thought is found in his Gifford Lectures, *The
Faith of a Moralist,* and in his essays "Theism"[2] and "Ancient and Medieval Philosophy."[3] The last two volumes we
have from his hands are the posthumous publications *The
Christian Hope of Immortality* and *Does God Exist?* About

the middle of his career Taylor became an Anglo-Catholic and from that time sought to present Christian Platonism as a form of "unreduced" Christianity which would be a genuine alternative for the mind and spirit of contemporary man. Like Inge and More he holds that we must accept and employ this distinguished legacy if Western civilization is to be lifted out of its present barbarism.[4]

*Taylor's Conception of the Nature and History of Platonism.* Like Temple, Taylor regards the thought of Plato as the essence of Platonism. Plato is the father of most heresies and orthodoxies in Western thought. His philosophy was highly original, and its influence may be detected in "the unconscious inheritance of the educated man of today."[5] The vitality of Platonism is due to Plato's supreme philosophical and literary power, and it courses pervasively through Western culture in the four main channels of metaphysics, ethics, science and cosmology, and natural theology. But behind the contributions of Plato stands the massive figure of Socrates.

In his *Varia Socratica* (1911) Taylor took up the thesis of J. Burnet's edition of the *Phaedo* and denied that the "historical Socrates" was merely the one of Plato's early "dialogues of search." Later he developed this thesis and held that Plato presented a faithful historical portrait of Socrates in those dialogues in which he is the central figure, including the *Apology, Crito, Phaedo, Protagoras, Republic,* and *Symposium.* The crux of this position lies in Taylor's interpretation of the theory of Ideas. First, neither Socrates nor Plato invented it; it was of Orphic and Pythagorean provenance and was taken for granted by both. Second, Socrates elaborated the theory and advanced it to the point where its difficulties were insuperable, as shown in the *Parmenides.* Third, Plato sought to solve these difficulties not primarily in the dialogues but in oral teaching in the Academy, by regarding Forms as "Numbers."[6]

Socrates is described as "an original genius in whose character there was an unique blend of the passionate lover, the religious mystic, the eager rationalist, and the humorist."[7] After the deliverance of the Delphic oracle Socrates became a man with the mission of insisting upon the supreme importance of "the tendance of the soul." His career reaches its end in martyrdom arising directly out of unflinching obedience to his calling. Socrates discovered the *psyche* as the seat of "moral personality." Thereafter, it was no longer possible to regard the soul as a Homeric ghost or as the fallen and exiled divinity of Orphism and Pythagoreanism. The conception of the soul as the seat of normal intelligence and character provided the basis for the apparently paradoxical doctrines of the identification of virtue and knowledge, vice and ignorance; the unification of the separate virtues; and the involuntariness of wrongdoing.[8]

Socrates found that the *archai* of the Ionians and the *nous* of Anaxagoras were at best only concomitant causes or indispensable conditions of an event. The real cause of an event in a mind-ordered world is that it is best that it should happen. Thus the foundation was laid for the teleological conception of the universe in Plato, Aristotle, and Plotinus which has become an abiding legacy of classical thought. Secondly, Socrates anticipated Kant in his moral argument for the immortality of the soul. The proofs in the *Phaedo* and elsewhere are not conclusive. Socrates' summary of the matter (*Phaedo* 114d–115a) is that the worth of the soul of the good man affords reasonable grounds for believing that death may be the entrance to a better life. Thirdly, Socrates was personally a mystic as the "Divine sign" of the *Apology* and the trance of the *Symposium* show. The basic conception which connects his moral philosophy and mysticism is that of deiformity. The *Sym-*

*posium* and the *Republic* together give Socrates' conception of the mystical way and end. Unless *Eros* be regarded as an *amor ascendens* it is simply a "mythological *bellum somnium.*" This path is not incompatible with dialectic. *To agathon* and *auto to kalon* are identical and together comparable to the *ens realissimum* of Christian philosophers. Knowledge of this is incommunicable since it is a direct vision; but the vision is impossible without the arduous, preliminary process of thought.[9] Essentially Socrates was concerned with the theory of knowledge in the broadest sense of the term: the problems of the relation of Forms and sensible facts. Such questions have not been answered with finality; still less has contemporary thought escaped the necessity of asking them. "The unique greatness of Socrates lies in the fact that he was the first man in the world to raise them with a clear understanding of what he was doing."[10]

It is Taylor's thesis that the most significant thing about the Platonic theory of Ideas is their "bringing together of the moral and the mathematical." Aristotle's synonym for a Platonic Idea—"the One over the Many"—clearly shows that Plato regarded it as the intension of a class-name. The various metaphors Plato uses to express relations of things and Ideas is comparable to Peano's use of the symbol ε, although for Plato the relation is not between the individual and the extension of the class. Ideas are self-identical essences which are never fully embodied in any sensible example, but are suggested by sensation. Since Ideas are not "thoughts" in the minds of Gods or men, the theory may be called conceptual realism. While they do not constitute a purely logical and aesthetic "realm of essence" like Santayana's, they are quite similar to Whitehead's "eternal objects" or "*recognita* amid events."[11] The only serious objection to Plato's Ideas is Aristotle's argument that as "separate" from particulars they are simply the hypostatizations of formal causes. But it is not enough that an Idea should mean only that one attribute is predicable of many subjects, since in mathematics and ethics the Idea is clearly Ideal, "a conceptual limit to which experience only presents imperfect approximation."[12]

Nevertheless, Aristotle gave a bona fide account of what Plato said in the Academy, where he constructively advanced the theory of Ideas beyond Socrates. In the earlier dialogues an historical individual thing seemed to be merely the temporary meeting place for a number of Forms, while the later dialogues (beginning with the *Theaetetus*) display an increased interest in particular sensible and temporal fact. There is less stress laid upon the sharp contrast between the eternal reality of Ideas and the transience of phenomena and more upon the real presence of intelligible patterns in the appearances. *Doxa*, while still tentative, steadily approximates the ideal of *episteme*.[13] Secondly, Plato developed the theory of Ideas in order to solve the problem raised by Zeno—that of giving an intelligible account of "surds" or "incommensurables." Against the Pythagoreans who held that extension was a mere aggregate of discrete units, Plato held that Ideas are not perceived through the senses, interposed *mathematika* between Ideas and sensible things, and said that the Ideas were composed of "the One" and "the great-and-small" or the "indeterminate duality" (*aoristos duas*). This latter is a continuum which includes surds. In making irrationals parts of a coherent system Plato laid the foundation for interpreting the universe in terms of mathematical physics, as in the *Timaeus*.[14]

Since Nature is always becoming, its arithmetization is like the evaluation of a surd which "never quite comes out," and physical science, even in its most rigorous form, is not dialectic. Plato's dialectic is comparable to the *Principia Mathematica* of Whitehead and Russell in so far as it consists of the "rigourous and unremitting task of steady scrutiny of the indefinables and indemonstrables of the sciences." But dialectic differs from contemporary logical analysis because it culminates in a direct apprehension of the Good as the source of both essence and existence. It is a teleological algebra and not merely a logical one.[15] Thus Plato brilliantly vindicated the rationality of the universe, and his thought suggests an alternative to the position of contemporary Logical Positivism, that moral propositions cannot be scientifically verified. Platonism rightly regards science to mean "inquiry into the systematic interconnections of truths"; and does not confuse the moral fact of purposeful living according to an ideal goal with a natural event. Plato believed that a critical metaphysic of all the sciences, including ethics, was possible.[16]

Where Socrates held that virtue is knowledge, Plato refused to reduce all mental activity to mere cognition. The *psyche* was neither an undifferentiated unit nor a congeries of discrete activities, but both a One and a Many. Since Plato took ethics, politics, and religion together as an intelligible whole, our present-day distinctions between them in his thought are artificial. In his earlier thought Taylor held that Plato failed to reduce the standing tension between ethics and religion, but later he finds that the concept of "vocation" (as in the self-sacrifice of the philosopher-king in the *Republic*) harmonizes ethics, politics, and religion, and shows that *philosophia* is both intensely otherworldly and severely practical.[17]

Ethics cannot be separated from politics because the State reflects the nature of its citizens. Furthermore, the State is also an educational institution which, if it is to be properly effective, must express in its constitution a true estimate of values. The Kantian conception of "practical reason" illustrates Plato's practical and otherworldly concerns. The *Republic, Politicus,* and *Laws* are not Utopian, but lay down a seriously intended scheme of reform for existing social institutions based upon the first full-fashioned philosophy of history in the Western world. Religion is related to this scheme through its position that man is a moral personality with an eternal destiny. While Plato's proofs of immortality are inconclusive, he taught that man has an inherent immortality. This belief enhances the seriousness of moral choice by pointing out that human destiny depends upon human character. Plato's myths in this connection are not to be justified because they "symbolize truths too sublime for rational comprehension," but because of their emotional effect upon the moral character. Man's moral task consists essentially in following the lure of the Idea of the Good which is *teleon* and *hikanon;* it is the vocation to deiformity, which is a *genesis eis ousian,* "a development leading to a stable being."[18] This phrase is the key not only to the interpretation of Plato's ethics but also of his philosophy of Nature.

In 1910 Taylor found Plato paying his debt to his Pythagorean teachers by putting his own discoveries in the mouth of Timaeus. Later he advanced the thesis that the science of the *Timaeus* is largely that of "a progressive Pythagorean contemporary of Socrates," that Plato originated little of it, and that it does not necessarily represent his own views.[19] Taylor interprets the natural philosophy of the *Timaeus* in the light of Whitehead's comparable doctrines. Both find that *genesis* or "passage" is the fundamental fact about Nature. Since Nature is always becoming, the results of natural science will always be provisional. For both the distinction between becoming and being, the sensible and the intelligible, does not involve a "bifurcation of nature." The *Timaeus'* question about whether the model is eternal or had come to be is parallel to Whitehead's inquiry concerning objects and events in Nature. Indeed, there is an "almost absolute equivalence" between the analysis of Nature in *Timaeus* 48e–52e and that in Whitehead's *Principles of Natural Knowledge* and *Concept of Nature.* While this is equally true of *Science and the Modern World* and *Religion in the Making*, there is no analogue in the *Timaeus* to Whitehead's "prehensions" or "Creativity."[20]

Taylor's second major interest in the *Timaeus*, which is combined with the first, concerns its theological implications. Since the sensible world is a becoming, it must have had a cause. This view involves the assumptions that the world may be apprehended as an individual whole, and that cause means "efficient cause" and not merely an antecedent event. The significance of the cosmogonical narrative does not lie in its mythical imagery, but in its doctrine that the world is "dependent and derivative, as contrasted with its uncaused and self-subsisting author, God." While the doctrine of *creatio ex nihilo* is not implied, Plato is committed to the position that the world had a beginning, although not in time. The world is a *gegonos*, not *aidion*. Unlike God or the Forms it is in the process of development, and has a history.[21]

The motive of creation was the goodness of the Demiurge, which is not, however, a personification of the Idea of the Good or of the *noeton zoon*. The Demiurge may be either an imaginative rendering of *nous* or it may be identified with the *ariste psyche* of the *Laws*. The Demiurge as *psyche*, molding the sensible world on the pattern of the intelligible, is the only reason Plato gives why Forms combine and how the sensible comes to partake of Form. Nevertheless, Plato was left with two unsolved problems which Plotinus later took up: the relation of a God who is not a Form to the supreme Form, and the difficulty of reconciling the conception of God as *psyche* with his eternal and immutable character elsewhere insisted upon by Plato—a God who makes both souls and Time.[22]

There is no finite God in the *Timaeus* because *ananke*, while a *planomene aitia*, is nonetheless susceptible to the persuasion of *nous*. There is no genuine polytheism in

Plato because *hoi theoi* are all under the sovereignty of a *theos*, "a supreme rational and righteous purposive agent operative throughout the whole of the universe." There is no "*de facto* teleology" in the *Timaeus* because *nous* which exists only in a *psyche* operates *ek technes*, and not by chance. The doctrine of man in the *Timaeus* involves neither a pantheistic emanationism nor a submergence of man in Nature. Human souls are not parts of the cosmic soul, but they are just as directly the creation of the Demiurge as the cosmic soul is. In the physical world a formless *chora* and the *paradeigmata* combine to give rise to *geneseis*, determinate processes; in the *psyche* the Same and Other produce, when blended, not *genesis* but *ousia*. Thus the parallel between the world and the soul is not complete. Plato recognized that the soul of man is neither simply temporal nor simply eternal. In the life of the soul the temporal and the eternal are "combined in the closest interpenetration."[23]

Plato held that there is a real affinity between moral and cosmic orderliness, and that both natural science and ethics arise from the distinctive human tendency, supported by the structure of the cosmos, to look for intelligible laws. In *Laws* X, 887a–899e, Plato formulated the fundamental principles of philosophical theology. Neither an imaginative nor socially useful fiction, it was a body of doctrines constructed upon a scientific basis for the socially useful purpose of founding citizens' conduct upon right belief. Plato's theistic interpretation of the universe is the "chief historical legacy from his philosophy to later ages."[24]

The heresies which Plato tried to refute by proving the Being, Providence, and Justice of God were atheism and the attribution to God of amoral or immoral characteristics. Plato's proof was *a posteriori*, and combined what were later known as the cosmological and teleological arguments. The sources of atheism are the mechanical corporealism of

the early Ionians and the Sophistic theory of the conventional and relative character of morality. Plato had to show
that the motions of bodies are all caused by prior movements
of souls, and that *techne*, conscious design, is the ground of
*tyche*, and not *vice versa*. *Kinesis* is universal, and is either
communicated or spontaneous. " 'Movement which can
move itself' " is both logically and causally prior to the
former; it constitutes the definition of the *psyche* in both
*Phaedrus* 245c–e and in the *Laws*. Inner psychic activities
are really ultimate and self-explanatory, and since no physical movement is spontaneous, the cause of cosmic movement
must be soul or mind. Souls may be either good or bad,
initiating corresponding orderly or disorderly movements.
Since order predominates over disorder in the universe,
there must be an *ariste psyche* as well as disorderly souls
which are inferior and subordinate. Taylor emphasizes the
originality rather than the finality of Plato's accomplishment. His proof rests upon three presuppositions which are
not generally accepted today: the universal validity of the
principle of causality, the impossibility of the infinite causal
regress, and the reign of law in the physical world. Furthermore, while the "best soul" is a perfect existent, the patterns
are metaphysically prior to it. Therefore, Plato's philosophical theology is not "fully theistic."[25]

Aristotle was a legitimate heir of the Platonic philosophical theology in so far as he held that the science of
God was possible, that it was the crown of philosophical
thinking, and accepted the argument from visible effect to
cause. But when he made God the "Unmoved Mover" instead of a "self-moving soul" he evacuated all ethical content from the idea of God. Where Plato founded an ethical
Theism, Aristotle is the father of a naturalistic Deism. His
solid advance upon Plato was his removal of God from the
class of souls, a "refinement" accepted by the Neo-Platonic
and medieval Christian thinkers.[26]

Taylor values Neo-Platonism primarily for its "thoroughgoing metaphysical theism" which had such a profound influence upon medieval Christian thought. Neo-Platonism was essentially the creation of Plotinus, and it must be regarded as a reasoned philosophy rather than a religious mysticism. Plotinus was a true follower of Plato who sought to solve the problem of God, which Plato left unsolved, on the basis of *Republic* 509b 8–10. Proclus' "Rudiments of Platonic Theology" summarize the principles of the Neo-Platonic school. Although Proclus was mistaken in his attempt to extract negative theology from the *Parmenides*, his discussions of the One, Causality, Progression, and Inversion have a permanent value for religious thought. The Good which for Plato was *epekeina ousias* was identified with the One which, according to Aristotle, Plato regarded as the formal element of the Forms. This doctrine made God "the absolute *prius* of everything," including Plato's Forms. And since the universal End was identified with the universal Source, Taylor has only to add the specifically religious concept of worship to make the Neo-Platonic doctrine of God serve as the basis of his own definition of Theism.[27]

This doctrine was amplified by the Neo-Platonic conception of causality. Known as emanation, it explains how the *hyperousion* One is related to the world. It is essentially a relation of *methexis* or likeness, and does not imply the temporal antecedence of cause to effect nor the logical relation of antecedent and consequent. Furthermore, it is not a relation between events, but a transitive relation between "substantival terms"—*to paragon* and *to paragonomenon*. When these doctrines are combined with that of *epistrophe* we have delineated that conception of "the real as a hierarchized system" which is fundamental to the Platonic tradition, and which was also a predominant feature of Scholastic thought.[28]

Next to Kant, Hume is the modern philosopher whom Taylor takes most seriously, because of his sceptical assault upon natural theology. The critiques of theism, expressed in Hume and going back to Lucretius, conclude that the alleged superhuman intelligence behind nature is lacking either in wisdom or in goodness. This argument is fallacious because it is based upon a hedonistic identification of good with pleasure and the supposition that the benefit of the human race is the sole or principal design of God. Kant, like Plato, is an inescapable influence. Also like Plato he finds the clue to reality in the interpretation of the moral life, but he does not call the result knowledge. Kant's moral argument confronts us with the dilemma that either the intelligible world is a moral order in which the highest good is realized, or the highest good is not realized and the conviction of its absolute value is an illusion.[29]

The thought of Lotze is the main historical link between Kantian Theism and the Logical Pluralism of G. E. Moore and Bertrand Russell, which Taylor regards as the chief contemporary philosophical alternative to Theism. Lotze's thought was Platonic in so far as he preserved the doctrine of transitive causality, held that becoming was real, and held that change was grounded in the nature of "M"—the world as a unity-in-plurality, a "living whole" analogous to the Neo-Platonic *plethos hen*. Russell preserves an "important half" of Plato. In the earlier portions of *Principia Mathematica* we find "the most potent weapon of intellectual analysis ever yet devised by man." The consequence for religious thought is enormous. If pure mathematics is a strictly logical development, and if all its conclusions are properly cast in the form of hypothetical propositions, then sense data are no longer necessary constituents of scientific knowledge. This disposes of the main ground for the denial that knowledge of God and the soul is attainable.[30]

But a more profound philosophy would preserve all of

Plato. Logical Pluralism insists upon a sharp dualism between relations which are universals and individual existents.
Since all existents exist only at a mathematical instant, there
is no causal change and no need for "M" or the *plethos hen*
to account for it. Logical Pluralism has no answer to the
question why some relations are actualized except that "it
happens to be so." This irrationalism is due to the artificial
severance of the realm of value from the realm of fact.
Unless the sciences of value are the merest trifling, the
Platonic-Kantian alternative must be adopted. The Idea of
the Good (God) is the source of both existence and essence,
fact and value, and "the most illuminating fact of all is the
*fact* of absolute and unconditional obligatoriness of the law
of right." Furthermore, the denial of permanent personality
for "an infinite series of momentary individuals" empties
personality of moral significance, rendering moral judgment
and duty impossible. The subjects of moral judgments must
be recognized as genuine, finite, historical individuals who
are complexes of actuality and *essentia*. *Essentia*, or real
possibility, is the factor in the individual's own actualization
as efficient, formal, and final cause. If it is true that the Good
is "the principle of actuality" (i.e., that the exemplification
of certain Forms is not inexplicable), then we are able to
maintain on a Platonic basis a cosmic teleology which takes
the form of ethical Theism.[31]

*Critical Remarks on Taylor's Conception of Platonism.*
Taylor's presentation of the Platonic tradition, and especially of the philosophy of Plato, as a whole is not excelled
by the other Platonists with whom we are dealing. However, his theory about the relation of Socrates and Plato is
untenable. Aristotle ascribes to Socrates inductive arguments
and universal definitions, and criticizes the theory of Ideas as
Plato's own.[32] Taylor's argument that Plato could not have
in the *Phaedo* misrepresented Socrates in a way "recogniz-

able as such by the very persons whom he indicates as the sources of his narrative" assumes that Plato was writing a scientific history of the Ideas.

Taylor contradicts himself and seriously impairs the value of the dialogues as a source of understanding Plato's mental development by exaggerating the importance of the oral teaching in the Academy. Despite the testimony of *Epistle* VII, 341c–d, without a fundamental emphasis upon the dialogues our knowledge of Plato's thought would be negligible.[33]

While Taylor uses the Christian concept of God as *ens realissimum* to illustrate how the Idea of the Good transcends essence and existence, he does not fully explain the difference between the two and tends to confuse these two different ultimates. In the *Republic* the Idea of the Good is not "above reason"; it is the purpose of reason to penetrate it completely. This is not true of the God of Christian thought, Who cannot be penetrated by the human reason. Generally a lucid interpreter of Plato's Ideas, Taylor seriously contradicts himself on an important point. Although he lays major stress on Plato's later interest in historical reality, he elsewhere says that Plato always kept *epistasthai* and *doxadzein* "radically distinct" and had no room for "the recognition of historical insight into the individual as genuine knowledge."[34]

Taylor distorts the Platonic teaching on immortality in making the case for it rest upon a "postulate of practical reason." Plato was fundamentally concerned with a rational proof for immortality, and with metempsychosis. From Plato's discussions of these topics Taylor extracts what seems to him to be the reasonable core, an inappropriate procedure in historical commentary. Although Taylor correctly points out the importance of the concept of *genesis eis ousian*, he exaggerates the importance of the role of the historical in Plato. Certainly in the *Republic* and even in the

*Timaeus* Plato depreciates fluent reality as against eternal reality.

While Cornford accepts Taylor's extensive and erudite accounts of the fifth-century scientific background of Plato's *Timaeus*, he rightly holds that Taylor's central thesis is wrong. Aristotle, Posidonius, Atticus, Plotinus, and Proclus furnish not "a single unambiguous statement that the doctrines of the *Timaeus* are not Plato's own."[35] Furthermore, Taylor's position on the *Timaeus* involves him in a serious inconsistency. On the one hand, the *Timaeus* is exclusively devoted to cosmology and natural science with mythically colored implications for theology. On the other had, Taylor holds that in *Laws* X alone Plato presents his "scientific theology." The strange conclusion to be drawn is that just where Plato is most scientific, his theology is most mythical.

Taylor's comparison of the natural philosophy of the Timaeus with that of Whitehead is generally both critical and illuminating. Cornford allows that the parallel between Plato's Forms and Whitehead's eternal objects is justified but that *to gignomenon* and "event" may not be equated, since that is to interpret Plato anachronistically in terms of the theory of relativity. But Taylor correctly points out that Plato's *gignomena* occupy duration and fill volumes, and are thus analogous to Whitehead's four-dimensional events. But neither Taylor nor Cornford point out that where the theory of relativity combines Space and Time into a single ultimate reality, Plato sharply separates the two. Time is the "moving image (true likeness) of eternity," while space is the formless *chora*. Furthermore, there is no genuine analogue in the *Timaeus* to Whitehead's Creativity. Souls are sources of spontaneous motion, the world soul binds and permeates and fructifies the cosmos; but neither eventuate in genuine novelty, as that term is understood today.

Cornford's contention that Taylor's analysis of the *Timaeus* makes Plato a Christian theist is unfounded. Taylor does use Christian theistic doctrines to illustrate Plato's meaning, but not to represent or embody it. Finally, Taylor does not stick to his novel thesis about the *Timaeus*, but inconsistently regards it as fully Platonic whenever it suits his purpose, as in his declaring that the activity of the Demiurge is the only reason *Plato* gives for the participation of the intelligible in the sensible.

Taylor's extreme emphasis upon the *Laws* as the exclusive source of Plato's scientific theology is unwarranted. The *Laws* bear more marks of being a "civil theology" of a pronouncedly moralistic kind than he acknowledges. Furthermore, he unnecessarily separates the *Laws* from the other dialogues, particularly the *Timaeus*. Despite mythical coloring there, the Demiurge is based upon the same assumptions necessary for the proof of the "best soul" in the *Laws*. Finally, he blunts the edge of his own thesis when he calls the theological tenets of the *Laws* Plato's "passionately held convictions" inspired by the personal faith of Socrates and Orphic revelational religion.[36]

It is unfortunate that Taylor's studies of Plato are marred by the distortions we have noted, since what is accurate illuminates the thought of Plato in itself, and in its connection with the subsequent Platonic tradition. As against Inge, More, and Temple, his Christian Platonism is more solidly grounded in independent Platonic scholarship. However, the fact remains that Christian Platonism needs a contemporary representative who can advance upon Taylor's valuable contributions without indulging in his fancies.

Although Taylor is correct in finding the source of medieval Christian metaphysical theism in the Neo-Platonists, his discussion of the matter is obscure. On the one hand, he holds that Plato's God is in "direct contact" with finite creatures, while Plotinus' One is as remote from the world as Aristotle's "Unmoved Mover." Thus the immanence of a finite deity is the basis of human-divine relations. On the other hand, he attacks immanence as the basis of "intimate personal relations" with God. The *principium individuationis* stands "outside the Universe," and only because of its transcendence are direct and intimate personal relations with it possible.[87]

Taylor's statement of the dilemma which is supposed to enhance the cogency of the Kantian moral argument is exaggerated. To say that there is either a moral order in which the highest good is realized or that the highest good is an illusion is contrary to the obvious fact that we may pursue and attain real goods which are neither the highest nor illusory. He also assumes that if Logical Pluralism is refuted his theistic alternative is established; not recognizing that a nonabsolutistic "principle of concretion" serves to rejoin the realms of fact and value. Apart from one essay, he is insufficiently critical of Whitehead's religious thought—particularly his doctrine of God. He predicts that future developments on the basis of Whitehead's cosmology will be "recognizably continuous" with "the Greek philosophical conception of the hierarchized universe, with God as its source."[38] This statement blurs the sharp difference between Plato's doctrine of God (to which Whitehead's is similar) and Plotinus' absolutistic One (which Whitehead rejects).

*Taylor's Constructive Religious Thought.* Taylor's apologia for Christian Platonism deals with methodology and three arguments for God, proceeding from man in nature, man as a moral being, and historical revelation. *The Faith of a Moralist* is concerned with the autonomy which any science may claim, and with the primacy which theology may claim. Our existence in the world presents us with problems with which we are bound to deal. The special methods of the various sciences are justified in that none of them can be simply absorbed into metaphysics. If this should occur, matter of fact would be completely rationalized and we would no longer have discursive sciences, but vision. Philosophy is the connecting link between ethics and theology. It asks whether seemingly chaotic existence has any unified pattern. It differs from theology because it does not rest upon authority, and it differs from the sciences because it is not preoccupied with special facts, and may, like Plato's dialectic, seek "even to destroy (*anairein*) the assumptions of all the other sciences." It is not the function of philosophy to give us "bird's eye views of the *omne scibile*" since the conviction of the rationality of the world, which it shares with science and theology, is strictly a postulate of the practical reason. It converges with all the sciences in so far as they seek to give a clear and coherent explanation of their data. Since the methods of philosophy are followed in natural theology, the crucial problem for religious thought is the justification of revealed theology.[39]

Philosophy and all the sciences are ventures of faith seeking understanding. Faith is defined as "voluntary assent to something about which you cannot *prove* that it is impossible that you should be mistaken."[40] There is no real opposition in principle between natural and revealed theology. *Quidquid recipitur recipitur ad modum recipientis.* The difference between the subject matters of the two disciplines is between what is generally disclosed at a "commonplace level of moral insight and practice and that which is directly disclosed to special recipients." The authority claimed by revealed theology should not be confused with inerrancy (*imperium*), but refers to *auctoritas*, the moral influence due to the dignity of its source. The data of theology have an authority comparable to that of sensations in physical science. In neither case can there be proof that the data are not illusory, and in both data and interpretation are intermingled. The given for both is an "implicit and dimly apprehended infinite" which analysis cannot completely exhaust. In the articulation of this datum initial apprehension is transmuted into recognition. This authority and experience are not antithetical terms, since the authority of experience is its refractoriness to intellectual analysis.[41]

But the problem arises, granted the validity of natural theology, is not revealed theology superfluous? Taylor defines special revelation as "an immediate self-disclosure, an inruption of the unseen order into the visible and familiar" which is not provisional but final. The intellectual formulations of special revelation are always tentative, although they may have abiding significance. The necessity for special revelation cannot be disposed of by arguing that the essential element of all religions is the moral one. Moral traditions are invariably related in terms of reciprocal interdependence with religious traditions. Furthermore, while (following Plato) religions must be morally tested, a theology is more than a collection of moral precepts, and the primary value of religion for life is not as a handmaiden of morality. The main object of attention in morality is the self and its tasks. But, historically, religion has proven to have had the most profound regenerating influence on conduct when God and His revelation is the center of attention.[42] Such is the basis of theology's claim to autonomy.

In his interest in the "events forming part of the great event which is Nature" Taylor follows the organic philosophy of Whitehead. On the other hand, he does not fully share in what Lovejoy calls the "revolt against dualism" and follows A. A. Bowman (*A Sacramental Universe*) in finding in the universe a "fundamental duality of modalities of being," the physical and the subjective.[43] He follows the philosophy of organism in so far as it is against the divorce, but not the distinction, between actuality and value; and he departs from it in so far as it denies the complete causal efficacy of the "dominant pattern." God is partially revealed in the causal and teleological orders which the inorganic and organic sciences disclose.

That Nature is relevant to theistic proof depends upon the relation of actuality and value and the historical character of all natural individuals. The alleged lack of connection between fact and value may be traced to Kant's first *Critique*, and amounts to a denial of the Platonic doctrine that *agathon kai deon*, the supreme principle of valuation, binds the structure of the existent together. In human life, value and existence are always distinguishable, but also always conjoined, as "the dominant features in the pattern of reality." With Plato, Taylor finds that the events of nature are *geneseis eis ousian*, and follows Whitehead in regarding the pervasive patterns in natural events as *universalia in re*, and value as " 'the intrinsic reality of an event.' " There is a whole complex pattern of the one world in which we live, and there are physical and personal subpatterns which reproduce "the pattern of the whole as *all*-pervasive." Subpatterns are interrelated, but analysis of any one of them will not disclose completely the pattern of the whole. *Per se* it is incomprehensible, but the richer subpatterns indicate its dominant features.[44]

Time is "the characteristic form of the conative, forward-reaching life." The route by which a configuration of points reaches a given shape may not matter to whatever further shapes it takes, but the route which an organism or personality takes is all-important, since it arises from its past and tends towards its future. Classical theories of Time from the *Timaeus* to Newton fail to distinguish between the historical and the chronological, with the consequence that the individuality of a thing depends upon its temporal and spatial location in an external container. Whitehead (and Bergson) are right in showing that each individual's concrete experience has its intrinsic temporal and spatial location in its life of interaction with its environment. The more genuinely historical an individual is the less will its destiny be determined by Matter and the more will it be determined by its own intrinsic character and relations with individuals of its own or a higher type.[45]

Although the physical and mental spheres are interrelated and interacting, they cannot be reduced to each other. Thus, consciousness cannot have emerged from the Nature from which it was originally absent, but is at least coeval with the physical world. Nevertheless, man is an individual, one organism lodging a unitary personal self. The fact that it cannot be proven that the personal self is derived from living matter suggests that its reason for existence lies in a "primary self." Mind is the condition which secures the frequency of "prospective adaptation," and unless it permeates all of nature, human purposeful life will be a highly improbable coincidence. Since man's mind causes physical events by design, then all physical events may have conditions "which do not themselves belong to the aggregate of physical events."[46] This argument from design needs supplementation by the moral argument.

In his earliest books Taylor sharply separated ethics and religion, but in the first volume of *The Faith of a Moralist* he is primarily concerned with the theological implications of morality. As in the Greek tradition, ethics should be regarded as "an inquiry into the character of the *summum Bonum.*" The Good is a Platonic *choriston eidos* although it is not directly accessible to our intellects. Since the Good is one, virtue is one. If there were, as G. E. Moore holds, an irreducible plurality of intrinsic goods, the unification of personality would be impossible.[47]

Man is a finite, historical, conative creature. Like Nature, his life is not only a *genesis*, but a *genesis eis ousian*. But his distinctively moral life is one of tension between the temporal and the eternal. To ignore this tension is to fall into either acosmism or naturalism. Furthermore, man is not only finite, but he knows that he is finite—a truth which secular philosophy ignores, and with it the tragic depths of the human spirit. But man is also free in the sense of being able to transcend his own particularity. His habitual behavior cannot be explained merely by conditioned reflexes, since he can modify that behavior by self-direction in the light of ideal ends. Nor is his freedom merely a natural spontaneity. Such a view would confuse the *liberum arbitrium* with motiveless choosing, and would obscure the minimum condition of moral accountability, which is "the ability to make an *impartial* estimate, correct or otherwise, of . . . two relative values."[48]

The moral life, however, necessarily fails of fruition apart from religion. Moral evil or sin is humanly *sui generis* and not generically animal, and guilt involves self-condemnation and a demand for punishment, as well as an indelible sense of pollution. Guilt would not have these characteristics if it arose from the mere breaking of an impersonal law. The subject of guilt is "the self I aspire yet to possess as my own." If the shame of guilt arising from disloyalty to our highest spiritual ideal is to be accounted for, we must think of this ideal embodied in a living and personal God. Since the facts of our moral struggle are the most immediately and certainly assured ones of our experience, the cogency of the theistic interpretation of the universe is immeasurably heightened, as against the entertainment of the "permitted" theistic hypothesis.[49]

Living and intelligent creatures, the richest of all subpatterns, can be understood only as subordinate and instrumental to the pattern of the whole. Morally and religiously, the discharge of duty is the road to deiformity. Since conscience is authoritative, a coherent theory of morality must presuppose the "categorical imperative." But that is not a sufficient moral criterion, because we do not possess the "reason" which the law of duty prescribes. It is communicated to us only in so far as we are faithful to prior revelations of it. While we cannot maintain the inerrancy of the human conscience, serious moral theory depends upon its absolute authority.

Deiformity, "the attainment of an assured and conscious complete personality," involves the conceptions of God as final and efficient cause, and immortality. Although God as an ideal end is too rich in content to be envisaged by man with perfect clarity or in other than a gradual way, accurate knowledge of God will transform us since our personalities tend to become like the models which our minds contemplate. Furthermore, since the moral task is essentially that of transfiguring the inward personality itself, the initiative to such an undertaking cannot come from the personality which is to be remade. The personality can be reconstructed around a new center (God) only in response to the initiative of God.[50]

Immortality is the culmination of the process of deiformity. It is not a state of indefinite duration but a quality of life. It is also a corollary of ethical Theism. The ultimate destruction of human personality would stultify moral life by making its eternal end unattainable. Despite manifold affinities between Platonism and Christianity on the subject, Plato diverges from Christianity by holding that man is immortal by virtue of an inherent part of the soul, that immortality is not a gift of God but is won through unaided human effort, and that the judgment of God is not final. Morally, Hebraic and Christian conceptions are more satisfactory. The doctrine of the resurrection of the body implies the salvation of the whole man, and not merely the survival of part of him. Grace supports a moral struggle which might otherwise end in despair. And the concept of the final judgment gives to the moral life the most momentous significance possible.[51]

The conative element of Hebraism, the emphasis given to the historical in the Christian *muthos*, the insistence of contemporary cosmological speculation upon the contingency and individuality of natural events all indicate that the purely philosophical approach to theological problems must be modified. At the minimum this means that natural theology must take the historical elements of the world religions seriously. At the maximum it means that the historical element most adequately supplements the speculations of natural theology. All of the positive religions have the essential characteristics of "historical origin, revelational character, authority, tradition, and institutionalism." Although it is possible to have a natural theology without the *credenda* which these characteristics involve, most natural theology arises and flourishes in the context of an historical religion. The crucial question for natural theology is whether historical elements are irrelevant or integral to a living religion.

Although discussion of this question is the theme of the second volume of *The Faith of a Moralist*, Taylor is most concerned with the doctrine of the Incarnation, which reconciles the tension between the temporal and the eternal which the study of the moral nature of man disclosed. Christianity gains its specific character from the "undemonstrated and indemonstrable conviction" that in Jesus Christ a human life was the transparent vehicle of the divine purpose. Although this is a walking by faith and not by sight, it is far superior to Gnostic attempts to "manufacture God . . . out of universals." These are bound to fail because reality is fundamentally concrete and historical.

Although Plato had more appreciation of the historical than any other classical philosopher, he was unable to attribute meaning to history as a whole. His cyclical theory of history also failed to do justice to the uniqueness of historical events and persons. The modern doctrine that the

arrow of Time is irreversibly forward-pointing enhances
the traditional Christian idea that history is a drama with a
meaning. Although Plato divined that the Creator took delight in the perfection of his handiwork, "even Plato does
not know that God loves sinners."[52] Faith in Christ secures
the Christian against what is, "in speculation, the last enemy
to be overcome," the paralyzing suspicion that values and
ideals may be futile, arbitrary, and fictitious. The catholic
Christian faith is vindicated by its possession of spiritual
joy, "a unique dominant quality" of new life on which
"the verdict . . . if it is to count must come from the men
who have first made it their own by living it."[53]

*Critical Remarks.* Instead of justifying theology's claim to
primacy, Taylor shows its continuity with philosophy, and
justifies its right to exist. His version of the cosmological-
teleological argument demonstrates as much as such arguments usually do: that there is probably a cosmic being
which bears a "remote analogy" (Hume) to mind as we
know it in man. The weakness of this argument lies in a
profound ambiguity in Taylor's metaphysics. On the one
hand he holds that the personal and natural are a "fundamental duality of modalities of being" which are "wholly
heterogeneous"; while on the other hand he holds that they
are "interrelated and interacting" elements of "the one concrete given process." His holding of these unreconciled
views is explained by his desire to preserve the traditional
Christian and Platonic this-worldly and otherworldly dualism, supplemented by the philosophy of organism. But it is
a supplementation by juxtaposition rather than by integration.

When Taylor uses the categorical imperative as the basis
of the moral argument he slips into a serious fallacy. On the
one hand he holds that the authoritative conscience is evidence which requires the postulation of the existence of

God in order to ensure a rationally coherent moral theory. But Taylor extends this legitimate argument beyond its proper bounds when he calls the authoritative conscience evidence which converts the "theistic hypothesis" into direct evidence of the reality of God.[54] Furthermore, it is difficult to see how a conscience which is admittedly *not* "inerrant" can be authoritative, and thus bear the load of theistic proof. Taylor also holds the self-contradictory position that while intelligent and moral personalities alone have "inherent and absolute worth," nevertheless man's ethical task is the "transformation of the self."

Taylor's greatest merit is his success in showing the roots, sweep, and continuity of the Christian Platonist tradition. He also attacks fundamental problems of religious thought without distorting Christian Platonism by going off on mystical or dualistic tangents. His greatest weaknesses are his antiquarianism and his lack of originality. Even where his antiquarian erudition is most extensive, his most original contributions (about the historical Socrates and the *Timaeus*) are actually untenable novelties. Essentially, he is content to adjust the thoughts of other men; and because of his massive burden of derivative thinking, he does not really make Christian Platonism relevant to the contemporary world. His religious thought is essentially a compromising apology, calculated to make palatable a traditional, middle-of-the road version of Christianity.

# IV: The Christian Platonism of William Temple

WILLIAM TEMPLE, son of Archbishop of Canterbury Frederick Temple, was born October 15, 1881, and died October 26, 1944. He was educated at Rugby and Balliol College (1900–1904). From 1904–10 he was a Fellow of Queen's, where he gave a course on Plato's *Republic*. In the Church of England he was ordained Deacon in 1908 and Priest in 1909. From the headmastership of Repton School he went to his first and only parish, St. James, Picadilly. From July, 1915, until 1918 he was editor of *The Challenge*, a Church of England weekly newspaper; and from 1920 to 1927 he was editor of *The Pilgrim*, a quarterly review of Christian politics and religion. Temple was successively Bishop of Manchester (1921), Archbishop of York (1929), and Archbishop of Canterbury (1942).

His early article, "Plato's Vision of the Ideas," was followed by *Plato and Christianity*. In *Mens Creatrix* (1917), where he sought to lay the philosophical foundations for a "Christian map of the world," Temple acknowledges as the chief influences upon his thought St. John, Plato, and Browning. *Christus Veritas* (published in America as *Christ the Truth*) continues the work of constructing a "Christocentric metaphysics." Temple's Gifford Lectures, *Nature, Man and God*, delivered at Glasgow (1932–34), present a "Dialectical Realism" to meet the challenge of Marxian Dialectical Materialism, and indicate the shift in his thought away from his former Idealism.

Temple's preparation for religious thought was more

philosophical than theological, and the Plato of the *Republic, Phaedrus, Theaetetus*, and *Sophist* was an increasingly pervasive influence. Temple saw Plato through the Idealism of Edward Caird and Bosanquet, both of whom were profound influences upon his thought. Later Temple regarded his earlier attempt to achieve a synthesis between Idealism and Christianity as impracticable, because of the irrationality of the world as it is. The Gospel is no longer regarded as the "clue to a universal synthesis" but as the "source of world-transformation."[1]

*Temple's Historical Conception of Platonism, and Its Relation to Christianity.* Temple follows the chronology of Lutoslawski and regards the *Protagoras* as the dividing line between Plato's portrait of the historical Socrates and the presentation of his own thought. He regards the works of Plato as a complete whole, and justifies his concern with Plato's living thought on the ground that he was the culmination of the genius of the Greeks. Plato's intellectual passion combined their predominantly rational and aesthetic interests, which are the source of most of what is viable in our thought and civilization "as distinct from pure religion." Through his inheritance of the Heracleitean physics from Cratylus and the search for ethical universals from Socrates, Plato "did more than anyone else before or since to open up all the questions with which the philosophy of religion has to deal." His originality is also indicated in his capacity to anticipate future developments, such as the Kantian theory of Categories and the Unity of Apperception (*Theaetetus* 184–86) and the Hegelian doctrine of Negation (*Sophist* 236–60).[2]

In his first study of the subject Temple held that Plato's theory of Ideas arose from the interaction of his logical inquiries and aesthetic intuitions, and an ecstatic experience associated with *paiderastia*. In *Cratylus* the theory is tentatively approached but not fully expressed, since the Idea is a teleological principle but not yet an independent entity. But since the existence of an *auto kalon kai agathon kai hen hekaston ton onton* is regarded as established in the *Symposium*, Plato must have had an "ecstatic vision" between the writing of the two dialogues. But this theory was "shattered" by the objections presented in the *Parmenides*, which were prefigured in *Republic* 595a–597e. The application of Ideas to all general terms leads to absurdities, and the *tritos anthropos* argument (*Parmenides* 130c, 132a) is applied with "ruinous effect." Plato tore his philosophy to pieces and in the *Timaeus* began anew, making the Ideal world part of a mythical structure.[3]

In *Plato and Christianity* Temple dropped his thesis about boy-love, and does not represent Plato as destroying his earlier thought. Rather there is a "great change," and the dividing line between the old and the new is found in *Theaetetus* 184–86, where it is pointed out that since the *gene* are applicable to the objects of all the senses, they cannot belong to any one of the senses. They belong to the mind, which is thus shown to be a unity in all acts of sensation.[4] Temple's final view is that Plato's Ideas were "transcendent entities," obviously related to the subject matter of the sciences which he knew best, mathematics and astronomy. Since the phenomenal and historical world did not correspond to this ideal of knowledge, Plato devised a static world of concepts known only by the mind apart from sense data and which was both the object of genuine knowledge and the real world—*to pantelos on, pantelos gnoston.* However, Plato was also concerned with the relation of universals to particulars, as illustrated by his demand for the insertion of the "How Many (*hoposa*) between the One and the Many."[5]

Temple appropriates several Platonic conceptions which are basic to his thought up to and including *Nature, Man and God.* The first of these is the Platonic ideal of philosophical knowledge, *eis hen epi polla oran*, which Temple calls "the ever fuller apprehension of the concrete universal."[6] This aim to discern what Taylor calls the "whole pattern of reality" is based upon the postulate which Temple sees as Plato's answer to the question of how any knowledge is possible at all, "the tremendous dogma of *Meno*, 81c-d—*hate gar tes physeos hapases suggenous ouses.*"[7] This conception of the "kinship" of mind with Nature (and God) is the fundamental epistemological postulate of Temple's *magnum opus.*

Temple interprets the Idea of the Good as the basis of the first genuine Idealism. It suggests that value is not divorced from, nor merely adjectival to, existence but that "value and value alone is substance or has substantial reality."[8] Thus, *Phaedo* 97d-e shows that teleology is the true method of explanation—a conception which plays a leading role throughout Temple's thought. Thus Temple comes close to the position of Taylor, which holds that Nature and History are best characterized as a *genesis eis ousian* for which the Good (God) is both efficient and final cause.[9]

Plato illustrates the fundamental reciprocal relation between the individual and society. In *Republic* VI–IX the constitution of the State reproduces the citizens' standards of value, while at the same time the citizens' moral sense is mainly produced by environmental influence. Plato ultimately subordinates politics to ethics because of the primary value of the individual's eternal soul; only his temporal concerns are sacrificed to the State. Since Justice in the State is an *eidolon ti tes dikaiosunes* (*Republic* 443c), and since the ideals of individual excellence and of citizenship are bound to conflict, ultimately the philosopher rather than contaminate himself will flee from the world (*Republic* 469d-e). Plato, like Spinoza, tried hard to find the religious foundation for politics but failed in so far as he lacked the modern doctrine of social development and the Christian motive of sacrificial love.[10] Later, however, Temple repudiates this depreciation of Justice as against Love, and combines the two. Christian charity is defined as "a supranatural discernment of, and adhesion to, *justice* in relation to the equilibrium of power." And he interprets Plato's *to ta heautou prattein* as the doctrine of Vocation, and makes it the basis of his Commonwealth of Value.[11]

Plato correctly discerned the ideal aim of both ethics and politics, and the form of education which connects them— *hena genesthai ek pollon*. Like Taylor, Temple emphasizes Plato's doctrine of the unity of the soul and regards the analysis of it into *epithumia, thumos,* and *to logistikon* as a descriptive phenomenology, and not as a faculty psychology. In emphasizing the initial multiplicity of the soul Plato showed the three primary relations possible in the State. A man may ignore, compete, or cooperate with his fellow-citizens. Whether men are motivated primarily by Desire, Pride, or Reason, a State will necessarily come into being. Temple and Taylor agree in interpreting the Platonic view of education, human freedom, and the disintegration of the ideal State. They also agree that the unity of the Idea of the Good involves the doctrine of the unity of the virtues, with the result that Plato closely approaches the essence of Christian ethics as formulated by Augustine, *Ama et fac quod vis.*[12]

Temple is closer to More and Santayana than he is to Taylor when he calls Plato a utilitarian in so far as he judged particular actions and principles on the basis of their usefulness. Plato's view is comparable to G. E. Moore's "optimific" doctrine of the right as that which is productive of the best possible consequences. In *Republic* 357b-d Plato divides goods into three classes, those which are intrinsically good, those which are productive of good, and those which are both. Plato and the ethical empiricists are right when they hold that the extension of the term "good" can be known only by experience. On the other hand, Plato was also an ethical intuitionist. The Idea of the Good, which is Justice on a cosmic scale, cannot be justified because there is no external or superior standard by reference to which it may be approved.[13]

In his earlier thought Temple attacks the problem involved in the paradoxical identification of virtue and knowledge, vice and ignorance. On the one hand, the intuitionist form of the knowledge of the Good implies direct and certain knowledge for the right ordering of conduct. On the other hand, moral values are not "determinable," and "Plato did not count himself to have apprehended the Idea of Good." Later, Temple would solve this problem by initially adopting the Socratic paradox, adducing together the doctrine of the emergence of mind from Nature and the Christian doctrine of Original Sin, and making mind essentially instrumental, but not ultimately effectual, in gaining the knowledge which constitutes virtue or salvation. Man's determination by his "apparent good" rather than by what is truly good is the ignorance which Socrates rightly identified with vice. However, since the whole personality is infected with this ignorance it cannot be removed merely by correct argument, and the initial Socratic insight needs further supplementation.[14]

Basically, Temple is concerned with the topic of Plato's anticipation of Christianity, and he illustrates what we have called the principle of maximum assimilation when he says that Plato came nearer to the truth of the New Testament than did the Old Testament.[15] That God is good, and the author of good alone, is the leading doctrine of Plato's religious thought (*Republic* 379a-c). This doctrine is compatible with that of *Timaeus* 29e and 41a, b, and closely anticipates the Christian attribution of Creation to divine

Love. *Timaeus* 92c 4-9 anticipates John I: 18, but in Plato it is the universe which affords perfect satisfaction to contemplation, and not the Incarnation as the disclosure of God. When Plato wrote the *Republic* we cannot be sure whether he meant that the Idea of the Good was personal, but certain passages of later dialogues (especially *Sophist* 248e, 249a; *Philebus* 30c; *Timaeus* 29e) show that he meant to identify his supreme principle with the living God. In *Theaetetus* 176a, b Plato reaches his greatest height with the doctrine of "resemblance to God" as the primary ethical and religious motive for man. However, Plato, like all philosophers, could not reach knowledge of God by discursive reason, since knowledge of the living God must come from religious experience.[16] Finally, Temple uses *Timaeus* 37d as the basis for a critical comparison of Platonic and Christian views on the meaning of history for eternity. Although for Plato Time is the "moving image" of Eternity, Eternity is so detached from Time that while history occurs because of its eternal ground, it actually makes no difference to it. In contrast to Christianity this view makes history metaphysically meaningless, but it is compatible with Christianity in so far as it holds that God's thoroughgoing transcendence of the world is the basis on which the universe may be explained and the religious impulse satisfied.[17]

Plato also partially anticipated the Christian doctrine of immortality. The authentic Christian doctrine of the future life holds that immortality is of religious interest only as an implicate of Theism. Furthermore, it is a doctrine of resurrection which is a gift of God, and not of immortality which is an inherent right of the soul as such; and it entails not so much final rewards and punishments, but declares "the inherent joy of love and the inherent misery of selfishness." While Plato's demonstrations of the inherent immortality of the soul are inconclusive, he does establish the truth of "the indestructibility of the spiritual principle in the uni-

verse" (*Phaedrus* 245c–246d). Although in *Laws* 959b
Plato holds that each soul is immortal in its own right, in
*Timaeus* 41a, b he holds that only God is immortal, and
that he bestows this gift upon his creatures. Unlike Taylor,
Temple accepts this as Plato's final view.[18]

Finally, Temple finds Plato's thought to be ambivalent.
When he speaks of the Ideas as separate from particulars,
he anticipated Plotinus' mysticism. When he speaks of
Ideas as participating in particulars, he anticipated Johan-
nine sacramental mysticism. It is basically in terms of the
"sacramental view of the physical world" that Plato anticipated the Christian doctrine of the Incarnation.[19]

*Critical Remarks.* In sharp contrast to Taylor, Temple's
discussion of historical questions in the Platonic tradition
is practically negligible; and yet his view of the historical
Socrates is in accord with the consensus of critical opinion.
Temple's theory that Plato's original vision of the Ideas
followed an ecstatic experience of boy-love, and that he
seriously held that Ideas were known *dia to orthos paidera-
stein*, is thoroughly demolished by Taylor. Boy-love has
no place in the curriculum prescribed for the philosopher-
statesman in the *Republic;* only in *Phaedo* 99d–100a is
there any account by Plato of the origin of the theory of
Ideas; and the language of initiation in the *Symposium*
(e.g., *exaiphnes katopsetai*) is plainly a symbolic expression
of the philosophical doctrine that after an arduous process
of rigorous analysis and reflection an axiomatic truth is
directly apprehended.[20]

The second stage of Temple's thought about Plato's
Ideas is almost as unsatisfactory as the first. To identify the
*eide* with the *gene*, and then to identify the result with the
Kantian theory of the Categories and the Unity of Apperception is an anachronistic distortion of Plato's thought. It
is not at all clear that he identified the *eide* with the *gene*.

If he had done so they would have become subjective, and it is very clear that Plato does not put the Ideas *in* the *psyche*. While Temple properly uses the words "meaning" and "truth" to suggest functions of Plato's Ideas, the words "fact" and "law" are misleading since those terms today imply what Plato meant by *ta phainomena* and the *hypotheseis* which were to explain them.[21] Temple also offers a highly conjectural, psychological interpretation of Ideas as the static mental objects of logical thought. In interpreting Plato's essentially objective idealism as the fountainhead of Western ahistorical pan-mathematicism, Temple distorts Platonism. Nature is an historical process for Plato because it consists of *geneseis*, and while he does have the mathematical ideal of knowledge, its method is analogous to the evaluation of a surd which never quite comes out. One reason why Temple fails to fully appreciate the role of *genesis* in Plato is that he concentrates too much upon the *Republic* where, indeed, change and becoming are exclusively associated with the phenomenal and unreal. As Taylor and Whitehead point out, this is not the case with the *Timaeus*.

One of the most peculiar weaknesses of Taylor's scholarship is the manifest sketchiness of his treatment of Plato's masterpiece, the *Republic*. Although Temple does not make this mistake, he does neglect the *Laws*. Taylor's interest in Plato's ethical and political theory is largely antiquarian, while Temple's analyses have more contemporary relevance. But when Temple says that Plato did not teach, but ought to have taught, that "man's duty results from his membership in society," he simply ignores a plain and important meaning of the *Crito, Republic,* and *Laws*. Taylor criticizes Temple's Anglo-Hegelian exaltation of the State at the expense of the individual in this connection, and Temple accepts the criticism, saying that "obligation is the correlate of value—absolute obligation of absolute value."[22] When Temple points out the "pragmatism" of the Socratic dialogues, he emphasizes a point which Taylor wrongly minimizes. Taylor's antipragmatism, which distorted even his interpretation of Platonism, is well illustrated in his pedantic reply to F. C. S. Schiller. When Schiller asked for an illustration of his contention that there may be a radical difference between truth and contradiction in propositions whose practical consequences area indistinguishable, Taylor replied by asking whether or not 9 is the number at the 100th place from the decimal point in *pi*.[23]

Temple's inability to harmonize empiricist and intuitionist ethical theories is illustrated in his directly contradictory statements in reference to Plato. On the one hand, he says that Plato was so preoccupied with the intuition of a transcendent Good that he became bogged down in an intolerable Utopianism, and was blind to the good elements in his society. On the other hand, he holds that Plato is not an idealist in the vulgarly depreciatory sense because many of his proposals were meant as a *reductio ad absurdum* of the Idealist method.[24] Both of Temple's interpretations are mistaken, since Plato was genuinely concerned with practical social reforms on the basis of full and accurate philosophical knowledge, as the *Republic* and *Laws* show in theory, and as the Sicilian ventures show in practice.

We conclude that Temple's discussion of the philosophy of Plato makes no advance in our knowledge of Plato, except as it incidentally corrects some of Taylor's errors. He oversimplifies the question of the unity of Plato's dialogues, scarcely recognizing the differences between them. In interpreting Plato's thought, he assumes that his meaning is plain for all to see. He underemphasizes the importance of some of the dialogues, like the *Laws*, and overemphasizes the importance of others, like the *Republic*. He does not use either the *Epistles* or the Oral Teaching in the Academy, and uses very little of the vast amount of research which has gone into explaining Plato's philosophical antecedents and the historical context of his thought. His treatment of the Platonic tradition, Christian and non-Christian, is brief and superficial.[25]

Along with the anachronism involved in asking whether Plato's God was personal, Temple erroneously identifies the Idea of the Good with God. While the former was for Plato what the *ens realissimum* was for many Christian thinkers, his God was nevertheless the Demiurge of the *Timaeus* and the "best soul" of the *Laws*. Again, the Demiurge is not suitable for illustrating God's transcendence of the world. Temple erroneously assumes that for Plato God and the Forms are alike eternal. Actually, it is in Neo-Platonism that God becomes the source of the Forms. The One of Plotinus and Proclus better illustrates the doctrine of the one-sided dependence of the world upon God which Temple clearly has in mind.[26]

Temple's treatment of the problem of evil in Plato is quite superficial. He is content with pointing out that there is a contradiction in Plato's thought between the Idea of the Good as the controlling principle of the universe, and his position that the evil things outnumber the good things in life. Although it is difficult to say whether or not Plato had any final solution to this problem, he at least carried his discussion of the problem further than Temple allows. In the *Laws* Plato infers the existence of the "best soul" because of the predominance of orderly motions in the cosmos.

We conclude that Temple failed in what he set out to do in *Plato and Christianity*. He has not made it "obvious" that Plato's works show a "definite anticipation" of Christianity. It is difficult to find any substantial evidence for Temple's belief that Plato was a "master-influence" upon his thought. Temple's attraction for Plato is best explained by his statement that Plato's "theory falls short of his intuition." He feels an underlying congeniality with Plato, because he thinks he knows what Plato meant even though

he ignores or disagrees with what he says. But this is essentially a philosophical predilection, insufficiently supported by historical inquiry and systematic reflection.

*Temple's Constructive Religious Thought.* In his earlier
thought Temple defines philosophy as the science of sciences which presupposes the competence of reason to grasp
the world as a whole. It is Platonic in that it seeks "to see
the One in the Many," "a vision of all time and existence,"
and "to follow the argument wherever it leads." Later
Temple insists that the essential function of philosophy is to
be a comprehensive science of real values. Scientific philosophy, which takes its start from the special sciences, is the
basis of the philosophy of religion which objectively studies
religious phenomena as a part of man's whole experience.
This discipline is essentially discursive and critical in method,
but it is constructive in that it may conclude that belief in
God is rationally validated. Much more so than Taylor,
Temple insists that there is a tension between philosophy
and religion because "the primary assurances of Religion
are the ultimate questions of Philosophy." Philosophy seeks
knowledge for the sake of understanding, while theology
seeks knowledge for the sake of worship. Both claim all of
human experience as their province, and each claims su-
premacy in it. Philosophy tends to explain facts by the
"lowest category," such as mechanism or organism, while
theology tends to explain facts by the "highest category,"
such as the divine purpose. Only this latter form of thought,
Theological Philosophy, promises to be completely satisfactory.[27]

The "sacramental principle" plays an important role in
Temple's thought. Avoiding acosmism and dualism, his
closest affinities are with Taylor. Temple adopts Platonism's
perennial feature of the "great chain of being" in regarding
the structure of reality as hierarchical. The grades of reality,

taken singly, are abstractions; since reality is a continuous whole, they must be regarded as real, broad distinctions within it. The first of the four strata of reality is Matter. In his early polemic against late nineteenth-century reductionist materialism Temple defined material substance as that with respect to which "other objects are without value or significance of any kind." The doctrine that Matter is the only existent and that it is determined by immutable natural laws is inadequate, because it is unable to explain how mind arises from mindless matter. Epiphenomenalism is a dead dogma if it be recognized that mind initiates physical activity as an efficient cause. The doctrine of the emergence of mind from Nature, which Temple adopts from Whitehead, shows that we first observe mind as consciousness of prior natural processes; hence we do not have to explain how the mind effects a transition from its ideas to an objective world. The philosophical significance of Materialism is that it opposes a cognition-centered Idealism, while it supports an experienced-centered Idealism. Its theological significance lies in the realm of sacraments. The express materialism of sacramental rites connotes a "sheer objectivity" which is lacking in an Idealistic conception of them.[28]

Temple's second major conception of Matter holds that it is an instrument of that which is higher in the scale of being—mind or spirit. Like Taylor, he regards psychophysical parallelism as inadequate to explain the relation between the two, and adopts a theory of interaction. "Spirit exists . . . by means of Matter; but Matter exists as a means to Spirit." Furthermore, Spirit is fully actual only when it controls Matter. By reason of this sacramental idea Christian Platonism, unlike Neo-Platonism or Buddhism, does not seek the spiritual by repudiating the material but would express the spiritual in the material, and seek the expression of Spirit in Matter. And only in this way, it follows, can economics and politics be humanized, and the continuance of religion as a powerful cultural force be guaranteed.[29]

In Temple's later thought the term "process" almost supplants Matter in his conception of Nature, while conceptions of Value remain paramount in interest throughout his
thought. By process Temple means the continuous becoming which is indubitably found in experience, and which
consists of successive occasions, giving rise to emergent
entities. An emergent entity cannot be accounted for by
its antecedents, by chance, by teleology, or by the supposition of perpetual creation. The emergence of mind can
first be discerned as a function of the organism in interaction
with its environment, consisting primarily of "embryonic
apprehensions." Far from being a portion of the "Royal
Mind of Zeus," primitive consciousness is an awareness of
feeling more closely related to desire and appetition than
to knowledge or purpose. Since mind first appears as an
organ for the satisfaction of physical needs, "Mind and
Body are one thing, of which the dominant character is
Mind so far as Mind is active." If this organic conception
be accepted, then the débris of modern philosophy resulting from Descartes's *faux pas* may be cleared up. If cognition is taken as the initial form of apprehension, then the
concrete variety and interconnections of actual experience
are minimized, with the results that the simple is taken to
be the explanation of the complex and there is developed a
subjectivism which does not hold that the world antedates
apprehension. Subjective dualism, in which Mind and Extension are set over against one another, leads to a denial of
objective reality to aesthetic and moral qualities, and of the
doctrine that "apprehension takes place within the world."[30]

Mind, the third stratum of the sacramental universe, illuminates the process from which it emerges and the values
with which it is ultimately concerned. Although conceptual thinking cannot keep pace with process, the emergence
of mind as an episode in process which can partially com-

prehend that process discloses that minds are not merely episodic. "The process becomes conscious, and then self-conscious, in some of its own parts." In his earlier thought Temple defined Value as "the element in real things which both causes them to be, and makes them what they are." Like Plato and Bradley, he argues that value is an irreducible mode of Being, and not merely attached to existence. However, Value must receive, or enter into, existence in order to be part of Reality.[31] Later Temple discusses value in terms of mind's emancipation from process.

Mind becomes detached from successiveness through the formation of a concept or "free idea." In comparing different possibilities of action, Mind regards as important the general qualities of objects, and not their particularity. The mind is further freed from process by the nature of its "present," or that portion of the empirical process which it immediately apprehends. Since the primary datum of experience is a continuum, then the "future" (concern with which is a basic characteristic of man as a purposive organism) can cause the past "while retaining its own nature, actually to be, in its organic union with its consequence, something which in isolation it neither is nor was." Finally, the mind distressed by the transitoriness of the world demands permanence, and thus discloses its twofold nature. In the apprehension of value as partially independent of the occurence in which it is found, Mind is most detached from successiveness. However, the fact that mind and the world are akin is the essential condition of value. The essence of value is Mind's discovery or recognition of itself in its object. Following A. A. Bowman, Temple finds that objectively real values are subjectively conditioned by the appreciating mind, which thereby actualizes what was potential. Value is recognized by the satisfaction it affords to the mind, although it does not consist of this satisfaction. The human mind's apprehension of value discloses a Mind which is more than any value. Since fact and value are given together in experience, and since fact cannot explain the origin of value, value is the "clue to the interpretation of the totality which includes both."[32]

Temple supports his "first dialectical transition" from a naturalistic philosophy of emergence to an immanent Theism by an analysis of the fourth stratum of the sacramental universe, Spirit or Purpose, and discussions of Truth, Beauty, and Goodness. Science, aesthetics, and ethics show how man's spirit may be partially fulfilled in the quest for value. These converging lines corroborate the distinctively religious quest which is continuous with them; yet in themselves they show that the quest of value alone cannot satisfy man's spiritual aspirations. Truth, Beauty, and Goodness, as desired ideal ends, all entail the truly adequate correlation of the mind with its environment. In the apprehension of Truth the mind recognizes a proper object of reverence, since self-deceit is not only self-stultifying, but is felt as "an offense against the order of reality." Man's sense of moral obligation towards Truth strongly indicates that the order of reality is not mere brute fact, but the expression of a personal mind.[33] The method of science is discursive and analytical, and it is restless until it achieves its ideal of omniscience. Practically, science postulates a cosmic order expressive of rational coherence. It studies things in time, and seeks timeless laws which describe or govern processes. The notional and static form of mathematical truth, which has been the traditional ideal of the will-to-know, has dominated philosophy with unfortunate results. It has led to a one-sided intellectualism which cannot achieve mastery of process. The desire of Truth cannot of itself truly emancipate man from process and control his behavior.[34]

Art and the aesthetic consciousness are the "natural culmination of Science, as Plato saw when he closed the argument with myth." By reason of its methods of intimate acquaintance with, and concentrated attention upon, its individual object, Art renders possible "an absolute apprehension of absolute Beauty such as is not possible of absolute Truth." In this perfect satisfaction of the contemplative mind, the transient is transcended, and the hope of mysticism is realized. By the creation of "essential symbols" Art reveals the value of the world. An essential symbol is defined as "a perfect case of the principle which it symbolizes," and it is the key notion of Temple's Christo-centric metaphysics.[35]

Goodness ranks highest in the triad of values, because morality is essentially practical and gains a more thorough mastery of Time than Science or Art. Furthermore, since the basic condition of value is the discovery by mind of itself in its object, moral considerations must take precedence over aesthetic or scientific ones, if there is a conflict, because the condition of value is fulfilled only when the mind's object is personal. The essence of personality (or spirit) is intelligent choice or purpose. Based upon animal mind seeking its "apparent good," spirit is fulfilled in "choosing between ends by reference to an ideal standard of good." Purpose is the activity of mind expressing itself through process. It alone is self-explanatory or intelligible in itself. Purpose is well suited to be an ultimate principle of philosophical interpretation and a true principle of cosmic origination because it is a reality which combines efficient causation with rational coherence. It avoids an indefinite explanatory regress and enables us to account for the origin of personalities. Purpose, as the highest category of the mind and the principle of unity in the world, when adopted as an hypothesis to account for cosmic process as a whole, is Temple's definition of Theism.[36]

Temple is well within the Platonic tradition in holding that man is a microcosm, and he regards Nature as both a vehicle of, and as an obstruction to, spirit. Man differs from brutes essentially in his capacity for forming "free ideas." The self or person is one by virtue of the unity of the organism, and its identity as the single subject of its experiences. This inner unity does not lie in an impervious core of ego, but in the whole psychic life. Man is a social creature, and fully attains his own unity through intercourse with other persons. Since personal unity is the actualization of one's capacity for integration, a person may be defined as "a self-conscious and self-determining system of experience." Human freedom consists of conduct governed by the whole person, and involves the absence of external coercion and internal compulsion. Self-determination is *sui generis*, because it is not the manifestation of the indeterminacy of physical *quanta*, but a spiritual determination by the apparent good.[37]

Like Taylor, Temple holds that human moral life requires religious fulfillment if it is not to be stultified. The distinction between right and wrong is an ultimate one. Absolute moral imperatives are manifest in the conscientiousness of the Will. To be conscious of absolute value and the absolute obligation which it imposes is "the most certainly universal form" of religious experience, and is of itself knowledge of God. But morality with its claims and counterclaims is self-destructive, because it presupposes the self-centeredness which it should overcome. If the whole of moral duty is to be expressed in a formula, then Plato's "Justice" and Bradley's "My Station and its Duties" must be replaced by the Golden Rule. "Love alone has absolute moral value." Science, Art, and preeminently Morality are involved in the quest for God. But their struggles are only partly successful, and finally indicate that man alone cannot satisfy his need for spiritual integration. In religious experience "God gives Himself" as the satisfaction of that need. Again like Taylor, Temple holds that religious experience is a given which is as authoritative as any other kind of experience. Authority and religious experience are not antithetical, but the essence of religion is "consciousness of authority and submission to it." Spiritual authority is neither coercive nor infallible, but in issuing from religious experience is continuous with all other forms of the apprehension of value, since it is essentially the Good evoking appreciation of itself. The distinctive contribution of religious experience to morality (and value theory generally) is its insistence that religion is essentially a worshipful, personal relationship with God.[38]

While there is a genuine unity of faith and knowledge, faith has the primacy because God is not known as an object, but by personal acquaintance. Belief in God is like an apprehension of universal import, and not like knowledge of a particular fact; and the authority which belief in God entails is like the scientist's conviction of Truth's claim upon him. Temple's "second dialectical transition" amounts to an attack upon the conception of God which Whitehead introduces as a partial explanation of the cosmos. Temple defines organism as the "notion of inner unification by coordination of function" and contrasts it with personality, which he defines as the "notion of self-determination by reference to an apprehended good." The difference between the two is comparable to that between a principle which is immanent and one which is transcendent. In the former case, a principle may be distinguished but not separated from the processes which conform to it. In the latter case, a person may be expressed in his acts but is nonetheless both distinguishable and separable from those acts. While Whitehead completely correlates God and the World and explains each by the other, he can only describe but not explain the complex totality which they together constitute. Like Taylor, Temple objects to Whitehead's making "creativity" a force beyond God, and holds that his cosmic optimism is misplaced since the facts of ordinary experience indicate that the universe is ambivalent.[39]

Temple does not sharply contrast Immanence and Transcendence as aspects of God since it is "the Transcendent who is immanent, and it is the Immanent who transcends." God is personal, but not a person. The metaphor, personality, is inadequate but nevertheless the best that we have, since it is the highest grade in the structure of reality that we know. To speak of God as transcendent of events is not to imply the conception of "a reservoir of normally un-utilised energy, but a volitional as contrasted with a mechanical direction of the energy utilised." To speak of God as immanent in events does not merely mean that a static principle is discernible in them, but rather a principle of perpetual variation or adjustment according to a consistent purpose. That ultimate reality is personal in this sense is the basis of the doctrine of revelation. While there are no revealed truths, there are truths of revelation, or "propositions which express the truths of correct thinking concerning revelation." Although general revelation in Nature and History is distinguished from special revelation in Christ, the principle which is common to both of them is the "coincidence of event and appreciation." Unless all existence is the medium of revelation, no particular revelation is possible; and all forms of revelation must be compatible with human reason and conscience. In so far as God and man are spiritual and rational they are of one kind, but the difference between them is complete in so far as "God creates, redeems and sanctifies" while man is the subject of these operations. It is upon an implicit Platonic basis that Temple attacks the major error of Barthianism, holding that moral progress is a reality which consists of "an increasing conformity to the Divine." Revelation, like the apprehension of value, occurs objectively but is subjectively conditioned. If the revelation is of a personal God then it must be in the

life of a person, since those who receive it can fully under-
stand only what is personal. Finally, perfect revelation occurs only when the Revealer and the Revealed are identical.[40]

Earlier, Temple held that the formula of Chalcedon was
"a confession of the bankruptcy of Greek Patristic Theology" because the presupposition of logical realism made
divinity and humanity into absolutely distinct substances,
and he proposed a treatment of the Christological problem
in psychological terms. He concluded that Christ is God
because he performs the acts of God. He is the "objective
event" which is the climax and standard of general revelation. No theophany, the Incarnation is the basis of the only
"tenable metaphysic" and presents history's decisive meaning. Since man's historical experience is not mere succession
but a "unitary apprehension of a successive manifold," such
a proximate emancipation from temporality indicates what
an apprehension of history as a single whole might be like.
The three major alternative ways for understanding the
meaning of history for eternity are the Platonic, the Pelagian, and the naïve religious view, out of which Temple
constructs his own synthetic view. The Pelagian view regards eternity as the simultaneous apprehension of the sum-
total of the temporal. While this view invests history with
momentousness as the arena of moral striving, it fails to recognize that process does not constitute eternity but is
wholly episodic in relation to it. The naïve religious view
emphasizes both the temporal and the eternal and has the
strength of a vivid and morally significant eschatology, but
it is too mythological. Temple concludes that the historical
and the eternal are reciprocally related, in that history
"makes a difference" to the Eternal, even though the Eternal
is the ground of the temporal. The ultimate meaning of
history is found in "the development of an ever wider fel-
lowship of ever richer personalities" which he calls the

Commonwealth of Value or the Communion of Saints. The concept of Vocation or Platonic Justice shows that each individual will contribute properly to the scheme of things only if each finds and fulfills his own place in that scheme. The spiritual world is both individualistic and communal, and constitutes a "Harmony of Harmonies" (Whitehead).[41]

Although in later writings Temple stresses the affinities of Christianity with Marxism (both holding that history is "the essence of existence") in his major work he was concerned to show how the Commonwealth of Value was the condition of eternal life and the standpoint from which the themes of sin and salvation are to be regarded. In *Mens Creatrix* Temple held that the nature of Good itself makes evil a necessary means to its achievement, and in *Christ the Truth* he held that the Incarnation shows how things which are evil in themselves can become "constitutive elements of the absolute good." In his latest utterances, he held that this type of explanation of evil must be deferred, even abandoned, for the sake of attacking the problem of eliminating evil.[42]

Evil is defined as Negative Value brought about by an alienation between the mind and its object. Intellectual evil, or error, is defined (following Plato, *Sophist* 254–58) as "a thinking what is not." It is symptomatic of the adventurous character of the mind's life; if there were no error, there could be no intellectual progress. Emotional evil or suffering is analogous in that it may further ennoble the basically noble character. Moral evil, sin, or self-will exists because it is the essence of Love to enter on "complete self-surrender to conquer the indifferent or hostile" and succeed.[43] This version of the *felix culpa* doctrine of sin is supplemented with the *sola gratia* doctrine of salvation. Abandoning the evolutionary account of the origin of moral evil as the survival of animal impulses in the rational stage of development, Temple argues that sin arises from the distinctively human capacity to form free ideas. For example, desire which is the organic basis of purpose may be so expanded by the imagination that it becomes misdirected, and hence leads to evil. Temple assimilates this doctrine with the Christian concept of Original Sin. The bias towards evil in human nature is such that man departs from his legitimate role of making value judgments and becomes the center and criterion of his own system of values. Since man is a social creature, evil spreads universally. The inevitability of sin does not entail the position that God is responsible for it; selfhood or finitude as such is not evil, but it is highly improbable that a finite self, by itself, will not be evil. Salvation, therefore, must consist of "delivery from self-centredness." The appeal of the Good is to desert self-centredness completely. Towards this goal real progress is possible, but it cannot be continuous progress, since that would be "an expansion of the circle of the self which is still the centre." The self's radical conversion and God's redemptive act are required if the self is to be saved.[44]

Temple's doctrine of salvation has an otherworldly focus and a this-worldly focus. Eternal life is of religious significance only in so far as it has the religious aim of transferring man's center of interest from himself to God. To his theological discussion of immortality, Temple adds the Platonic conception that man is naturally capable of immortality. This is based upon the mind's capacity to form free ideas, to be determined by its apparent good, and to achieve an increasing, although always proximate, independence of the physiological organism.[45] In his earlier thought Temple held that the "crucial problem of human life is to acquire detachment from the present and to become rooted in the Eternal," but under the impact of contemporary events and ideologies he insists that religious thought must make a many-sided effort to grapple with pressing social, political, and economic problems. In one of his latest statements we read of five basic decisions which outline his position. The first is a decision for God who has revealed Himself in Nature, History, the prophets, and Christ. Such a decision gives faith an aggressive and effective spiritual power which sentimental theism and rationalistic deism lack. Secondly, a decision for human sociality would "create a new epoch" in history. The next two decisions concern acknowledgment of man's roots in Nature and History. Finally, there is required a decision for the Gospel and the Church as the basis and vehicle of God's will for man. The present cultural crisis of the West is due to the "fragmentation" of life. To cure this the Church should not merely insist upon ideals, since there is no such thing as a Christian social ideal immediately applicable to contemporary society. Love and Justice should be regarded rather as "regulative of our application of other principles than taken as immediate guides to social policy." The cure lies in the direction of reestablishing a unity between "men's ultimate beliefs and habits and their conscious aims." For this task the Christian religion offers a well-tested principle of integration.[46]

*Critical Remarks and Conclusion.* When Temple says that "Matter exists in full reality but at a secondary level" he is vainly attempting to reconcile the two different conceptions of Matter we have traced in his thought, and falling into a metaphysical inconsistency similar to Taylor's. Matter or process as fully real implies that it has existential priority to the mind or spirit which emerges from it. At this point Temple adheres to a form of naturalism analogous to Alexander's or Whitehead's. But when Matter is also said to exist at a secondary level, spirit has the existential and teleological priority, and Temple's thought takes the form of a spiritualistic idealism. Temple correctly points out that Christianity is the "most avowedly materialistic of all the great religions" because it believes in the ultimate significance of the historical process, and in the reality of matter and its place in the divine scheme. This gives to Christianity a relevance to man's mundane concerns which Inge's mysticism and More's dualism denies it. However, except where he adopts Whitehead's view of process, Temple has an outmoded conception of Matter as the inert, indeterminate substratum of all existents. He is not aware of the significance of the Platonic surrogate for Matter—the Receptacle.

Temple discusses in a very superficial way the second stratum of his hierarchical universe—Life. It simply means nascent mind, and his main concern is to show that the emergence of mind from process is the most noteworthy single fact about process. His view that it is the historical individual, and not the race, which develops is close to Taylor's view of process as a *genesis eis ousian*. But Temple's desire to replace Logic with the History of Philosophy as the fundamental discipline of the mind is more Hegelian than Platonic. However, Temple's broad use of the word Logic as *logos*, or dynamic world-structure, is identical with Taylor's conception of the "pattern of the whole" as discernible among the courses of historical individuals. But neither conception should be confused with Plato's Idea of the Good, as both Temple and Taylor tend to do, since that is a *choriston eidos* ultimately accessible to man's reason, while the Christian God is a personal being known by man through His self-disclosure.

Temple's conception of Value as "objectively real, but subjectively conditioned" does justice to the Platonic conception of values and to the emphasis in modern philosophy upon the creative contribution of man's mind to his knowledge, but it does not save him from a serious contradiction. On the one hand he holds with Bradley that every man's sense of value is ultimate. This individualistic form of the *homo mensura* doctrine is both anti-Platonic and self-contradictory. For Temple elsewhere holds that worship itself is comparable to an education in value judgment in which we pass from "the subjective judgment 'This pleases me' to the objective judgment 'I find this good.' "[47]

To designate that with which mind finds itself akin in its environment Temple uses the phrase "another Mind or Somewhat akin to Mind." The latter is an impersonal *logos*, rational or aesthetic pattern, which the mind finds in experience. Such a conception is a presupposition of all serious thought. If mind and nature are not homologous, if there is no integral connection between the two, there can be no reliable knowledge. But Temple's conception of "another Mind" is definitely a form of personalistic Theism. He confuses these two different conceptions, instead of keeping them distinct and indicating the precise ground of transition between them.[48] Temple's conception of Value is also confused. On the one hand he says that Truth, Beauty, and Goodness are inherent and absolute values. Without any notice of inconsistency he proceeds to say that "the One Absolute Value, of which these three are forms, is Love," and also ranks Truth, Beauty, and Goodness in an ascending order of worth.[49]

Temple's argument from the human sense of moral obligation towards Truth to the order of reality as the expression of a personal mind is a keen one. It is spoiled, however, by the fact that it is not necessary to say that the order of reality is *either* a "brute fact" *or* the expression of a personal mind since it may be, as he himself points out, "a Somewhat akin to Mind." Temple's appeal to Plato in seeking to show the superiority of Art to Science is without foundation. As Taylor points out, both Science and Art are unfinished, and Plato in the *Symposium* "makes the ascent *from* Art through Science to something which is better than both."[50] To say that Goodness alone among all the values is a "human creation" not only deprives it of objectivity, but has no foundation in Platonism and very little in Christianity. Like Taylor, Temple is caught in the difficulty which arises when one attempts to combine Kantian moral idealism with a Christian doctrine of salvation. Man has an "inherent and ultimate value" but that is not sufficient to guarantee the realization of the moral ideal of perfect self-determination. To be consistent Christianity must say that God alone has, or is, ultimate value.

In his earlier writings Temple thought that his Anglo-Hegelian Idealism was thoroughly supported by Platonism. Actually his understanding of Platonism was falsely colored by his Idealism, inasmuch as he stressed synthesis and spiritualism to the neglect of Platonism's concern with analysis, and realistic and organic conception of the physical world. Both Temple and Taylor are learned apologists for the Christian faith, but they differ in aim and method. Taylor uses "philosophical theology" to show that the Christian faith is not inherently unreasonable. Temple continually subordinates philosophy to theology, and in his latest thought he was so concerned with theology that philosophy became irrelevant. Temple's superiority to Taylor is threefold. He was more sensitive to the pressing problems of contemporary man, and saw that cataclysmic social changes required radical revisions of traditional thinking. On a fundamental level he sought to synthesize creatively leading themes of classical, Christian, and modern thought. His thought expresses a profounder religious spirit than Taylor's because he emphasized the importance of worship as a vital act. Towards the end of his career Temple came closer to expressing the full religious genius of Christianity in its contemporary relevance than any other Christian Platonist. But, while Temple recognizes most of the changes in his thought, he is not sufficiently reflective about them. There is very little evidence that he was concerned with the problem of the relation of his former explicit Platonism to his changed world-view. And surely it was a defection from the rationality of Platonism not to have more fully explored the theoretical reasons for the changes in his thought.

Taken together, and compared to Inge and More, Taylor and Temple represent a valuable contribution to the contemporary phase of Christian Platonism. Neither one-sidedly mystical nor dualistic in outlook, they recognize that historically and systematically Platonism and Christianity are integrated on the basis of their ethical Theism. This conception distorts neither the religion of the Bible nor the religious thought of the dialogues. They also recognize that Christianity gives added religious momentousness to the Socratic-Platonic conception of the soul as the moral personality. They are cognizant of the Hebraic heritage of Christianity and open to the doctrines and insights of contemporary philosophy and natural science in their recognition of the importance of Nature and History. However, Taylor (following Whitehead too closely) tends to exaggerate Platonism's concern with Nature and History, while Temple (following Whitehead too closely without adequate recognition of his Platonic presuppositions) tends to depreciate Platonism's concern with Nature and History. Although their errors are less serious than More's anti-naturalistic dualism and Inge's anti-historical acosmism, these comparisons indicate that the Christian Platonism of the future must try to construct more satisfactory doctrines of Nature and History.

# V: Platonic Themes in Whitehead's Religious Thought

ALFRED NORTH WHITEHEAD was born February 15, 1861, at Ramsgate on the Isle of Thanet, Kent, and died in December, 1947. The son of an Anglican clergyman, he was educated at Sherborne, Dorsetshire (1875–80), and at Trinity College, Cambridge, where he remained as scholar and fellow from 1880–1910. His intellectual life may be divided into three periods. In the first period he was concerned with various branches of mathematical study, including algebra, geometry, and the logical analysis of the foundations of mathematics. His first book was *A Treatise on Universal Algebra* (1898), and the most notable achievement of the period was the *Principia Mathematica*, which he did in collaboration with Bertrand Russell. From 1911 until 1914 Whitehead held various positions at University College, London; and from 1914 until 1924 he held a professorship at the Imperial College of Science and Technology at Kensington. It was during this second period that he was most concerned with natural philosophy, as shown in his *An Enquiry concerning the Principles of Natural Knowledge, The Concept of Nature*, and *The Principle of Relativity*.

At the age of sixty-three Whitehead became Professor of Philosophy at Harvard University, holding this position from 1924 until 1937. During this period, and until his death, Whitehead produced those works which show his interest in speculative, Platonic, and religious thought. In his two series of Lowell Lectures, *Science and the Modern*

*World* and *Religion in the Making,* he broaches some of the themes which are more fully explored in his Gifford Lectures, *Process and Reality,* delivered at the University of Edinburgh in 1927-28. *Adventures of Ideas,* which Hocking has called Whitehead's "happiest" book, is a general discussion of the Platonic influence in Western thought. Two of his essays, "Mathematics and the Good" and "Immortality," summarize the basic ideas of his thought as they became clarified in the course of its development.

A. A. Bowman stresses Whitehead's hylozoism; Erich Frank and F. S. C. Northrop emphasize his Bergsonianism; Victor Lowe detects the strong influence of Wordsworth. Whitehead himself speaks of the authoritative influence of the great Western philosophers upon his thought; and of these the greatest is acknowledged to be Plato. "The safest general characterization of the European philosophical tradition is that it consists of a series of footnotes to Plato."[1]

*Whitehead's Conception of Platonism.* Whitehead regards the Pythagorean notion of "a direct intuition of a righteousness in the nature of things, functioning as a condition, a critic, and an ideal," as the basis of subsequent Greek attempts to formulate a rational religion. This is seen as following from Pythagoras' insistence upon the utmost generality in reasoning whereby he initiated the thus far unresolved debate concerning the status of mathematical entities in the realm of things. Despite the crudity of Pythagoras' formulation of the role of such entities in perceptual experience, the impact of his main thesis was enormous. The Platonic theory of Ideas is a revision and refinement of Pythagorean number theory. Plato and Pythagoras established the paradox, confirmed by the history of modern science, that "the utmost abstractions are the true weapons with which to control our thought of concrete fact."[2]

Whitehead stresses the perennial importance of Plato. His

greatness as a metaphysician lies in the profound intuition which he displayed, and not in his attempts at systematization in which he failed. His dialogues are the foundation of European philosophy and are still freshly suggestive because he raised fundamental questions without offering answers with the pretense of dogmatic finality. While Plato occasionally betrayed his own insight (as in *Laws* X where he justified religious persecution), his thought was essentially heuristic, especially in the use of novel verbal formulations to express hitherto neglected aspects of reality. Nevertheless, Plato's comprehensive, theoretical reason which he "shares . . . with the Gods" must be supplemented by reason in action which Ulysses "shares . . . with the foxes."[8]

While Whitehead condemns servile imitation of the Greeks as most unlike them, he holds that the ultimate problem of metaphysics is the conception of a complete or, as Plato puts it, *panteles* fact. We are then driven to conceive the fundamental notions about the nature of reality. Plato found seven of these: Ideas, Physical Elements, the Psyche, Eros, Harmony, Mathematical Relations, and the Receptacle. The interrelations of these notions comprise the texture of all philosophical systems. While we cannot identify modern concepts with those of Plato there are definite analogies between them.[4] Thus, when Plato in the *Timaeus* referred to that which is "always in the process of becoming and perishing and never really is," when he argued in the *Sophist* that "not-being is itself a form of being," he raised the hitherto insufficiently recognized problem of "perishing" as an aspect of process.[5]

What is generally regarded as Whitehead's most important appropriation from Plato is his doctrine of "eternal objects" or entities which may be conceptually recognized without necessary reference to temporal actuality. Plato regarded Ideas generally as independent and absolutely real existents which constituted a static, timeless, and completely self-sustaining realm. When he regarded the world of flux as definitely excluding many relevant ideal possibilities, he inaugurated the unfortunate dualistic tendency of European philosophy and paved the way for Positivism's view of the phenomenal world as irrational. Qualitative and quantitative abstractions are mere fantasies unless they essentially refer to process. However, Plato did make his Ideas essentially referent to process, as in the commingling of the *genera* (*Sophist* 253c–d). Thus Plato anticipated the conception of an Idea as a bridge between "the mortal world of transitory fact acquiring the immortality of realized value; and . . . the timeless world of mere possibility acquiring temporal realization." In the dipolarity of mental and physical experience, every occasion has a definite *form of* experience and a definite *form for* realization, which Whitehead identifies with Platonic Ideas.[6]

Whitehead defines Plato's Psyche as "the agency whereby ideas obtain efficiency in the creative advance," and identifies it with his own doctrine of the "primordial nature of God." Plato regarded the Demiurge as the supreme persuasive agency in the universe. In the human response to this agency there is marked the difference between a communal and a rational religion. In the former God is a cosmic tyrant who must be appeased for the sake of self-preservation, while in the latter He is a divine companion to be imitated. While Plato wavered between these two conceptions of God, his basic view was that the divine persuasion is the foundation of cosmic order, which produces whatever harmony is possible amid brute forces. Plato's conception of the human Psyche was a general idea which was given exemplification by Christianity, as "a prophecy which procures its own fulfillment." Furthermore, since Plato regarded psychic factors in the universe as the source of all spontaneity, he laid the metaphysical foundation for social freedom as the preeminent quality of civilization.[7]

Whitehead defines Plato's Eros as the Psyche's spontaneous urge towards the realization of ideal perfection and Nature's tendency towards self-harmonization. Plato's Eros shows that he was no mere rationalist since the entertainment of Ideas is intrinsically associated with an inner ferment of subjective feeling which is both an immediate enjoyment and an appetition. Here Whitehead believes Plato to have anticipated his own doctrine of "prehension" as well as Bradley's doctrine of Feeling. Because Plato did not separate vital emotion from bare cognition and held that the whole of man's character conforms to the adequate knowledge which he possesses, he successfully identified virtue and knowledge.[8]

Whitehead describes Plato's Receptacle as "the general interconnectedness of things" which transforms plurality into unity, without any precise determination of mutual relationships. As the matrix of Becoming it is analogous to the Space-Time of modern mathematical physics. The Receptacle explains how the plurality of physical actualities are components in each other's natures and is thus the basis of the doctrine of Immanent Law. The doctrine of mutual immanence was also prefigured in Plato's doctrine of Being which, in Sophist 247e, he defined as "power." The doctrine that the essence of being is to be implicated in causal action on other beings provides the most adequate doctrine of causation, since it gives a basis for the connexity of the world and the transmission of its types of order. The Platonic definition of Being as "power to make a difference" Whitehead calls the "ontological principle," or the principle of efficient and final causation, which holds that "the reasons for things are always to be found in the composite nature of definite actual entities— . . . no actual entity, then no reason." The revised Platonic conception of causation shows the way to escape the destruction of traditional formulations of the cosmological argument. Comparing the Timaeus and

Newton's *Scholium*, Whitehead observes that Plato suggests the prominence of Becoming in Nature, a view compatible with modern evolutionary theory. Newton, on the contrary, regarded Nature as a fully articulated system of supernatural origin. A valid cosmological argument is impossible on Newton's basis because causation concerns actualities within the world, and to extend it to an entity which transcends the world is illegitimate. Newton's "Semitic" theory of creation did not provide for the evolution of matter, with the result that the material universe and its present type of order was eternal. Against this Whitehead proposes the *Timaeus'* theory of organic evolution in which creation is not "the beginning of matter of fact, but the incoming of a certain type of social order."[9]

Like Taylor, Whitehead regards Plato's greatest contribution to the philosophy of science to lie in his mathematical approach to scientific problems. Unlike the cosmology of Epicurus in which the paths of the atoms are arbitrary, or Newton's separation of the formal nature from the behavior of things, Plato held that a thing's behavior is a function of its mathematical and dynamic character. "Newton would have been surprised at the modern quantum theory and at the dissolution of quanta into vibrations; Plato would have expected it."[10]

While for Plato (and Aristotle) the Good is an ultimate which cannot be analyzed in terms of things more ultimate than itself, his doctrine of harmony holds that right proportions should obtain among the several components of composite things. The concept of Harmony shows that mathematics and ethics are intimately related because "activity means the origination of patterns of assemblage" which are not only the province of mathematics but also of ethics, because man's control of purposes depends upon his understanding of patterns in their various applications. Furthermore, mathematical concepts and ethical ideals both reveal man's distinctive capacity for abstract thought about things apart from their immediate exemplification or realization. In the present revolutionary era tradition has lost its compelling force. Contemporary man requires a rational vision of the world, which would afford the knowledge that Plato identified with virtue. Whitehead observes that Plato held that the ideal Republic was immediately present to the consciousness of the wise in the temporal world, and ventures the prophecy that the successful religion of the future will be the one which can make clear "some eternal greatness in the passage of temporal fact."[11]

As Aristotle imposed his systematic thought upon his Platonic inheritance, he corrected the static aspect of Platonism by his analysis of generation. In contrast to the *Timaeus'* doctrine of the World Soul as an emanation (which led to the puerilities of Gnosticism), Aristotle's Prime Mover illustrates the type of deity which a genuine metaphysics requires. The gravest difficulty of the Aristotelian metaphysics lies in the doctrine of Primary Substance as "the ultimate substratum which is no longer predicated of anything else." Against this doctrine Whitehead argues that substances are to be found in events, or genuine temporal and spatial *relata*. Space and Time cannot be regarded as the containers of events, and primary substances cannot be regarded as ultimately disjoined, because every experiencing subject interprets its experience as indicative of its being in a real community with other realities. Whitehead supplants Aristotle's doctrine of Primary Substance with the metaphysical ultimate of "Creativity," which is partly based upon Plato's Receptacle and Being. Finally, it is the Christian theologians of Alexandria, and not Aristotle, who fundamentally improved upon Plato's metaphysics.[12]

Christianity is based on historical events scattered within the twelve-hundred-year period between the Hebrew prophets and Augustine. As a whole, it began in barbarism and ended in failure. Although a "re-formation" of Christianity is possible, its contemporary decadence is due to its barbaric heritage. The first phase of the Christian epoch was signalized by Plato's great religious discovery that God is immanent in the world persuasively and not coercively. The second phase, which constitutes the driving power of Christianity, is "primarily an exhibition in life of moral intuition, with a sufficiency of intellectual insight to give an articulate expression of singular beauty." The conjunction of the Platonic intuition and the Christian exemplification (in origin historically independent) constitutes the essence of religion as "the vision of something which stands beyond, behind, and within, the passing flux of immediate things." This vision claims only worship, or "assimilation urged with the motive force of mutual love." For this reason, the life of Christ as the exhibition of gracious power has "the decisiveness of a supreme ideal."[13]

The barbaric alternative to this Platonic and Christian conception arose in despotic social systems, and held that God was a cosmic tyrant. The metaphysical sublimation of this notion consists in attributing "eminent reality" to God. Christian theology had an opportunity to improve upon this conception, in terms of the Platonic doctrine of mutual immanence, which would have enabled the doctrine of God to survive the onslaughts of Hume's *Dialogues*. But the efforts of the Christian Platonists of Alexandria ended in failure because they were not thoroughgoing enough in their metaphysics. In reverting to the Semitic doctrine of God as transcendent, they left a gulf between God and the world. Since God was omnipotent, he was also responsible for evil. Since God was excluded from complete metaphysical rationalization, it was impossible to prove that He existed. Theistic proofs must begin with the actual world, and they cannot discover anything not included in the world which nevertheless explains it. Plato grounded the relation of God

and his envisagement of Ideas to the world in terms of "mere
dramatic imitation." The World Soul as an *eikon* obscured
the ultimate question of the relation of permanent and fluent
reality and posed the "ultimate platonic problem." This
problem arises from the separation of flux from permanence
and makes the notion of illusion a fundamental philosophical
principle. A sound metaphysics would show that unity and
plurality, God and the world, flux and permanence are related to one another strictly in terms of mutual immanence.
This problem came to the theologians of Alexandria (and
Antioch) in a highly specialized form. Thus, in the doctrine
of the Trinity they proposed a solution based on mutual
immanence which held that there is "a multiplicity in the
nature of God, each component being unqualifiedly divine."
This solution was an advance upon Platonism as far as it
went, but it was finally inadequate because the doctrine of
mutual immanence was not applied to all actualities. By ex-
empting God from the categories applicable to temporal
actualities, they made Him eminently real and the world
derivatively real.[14]

Whitehead's insistence that theological concepts be included within the scope of metaphysics entails an attack
upon Positivism. Bentham's Utilitarianism and Comte's
Positivism uncritically regarded "generalized emotions" derived from two thousand years of Platonism and Christianity
as "ultimate moral intuitions, clear matter of fact." But in
discarding metaphysics they did not preserve their own
doctrines from vulnerability to scepticism. "They have
gained nothing in the way of certainty by dropping Plato
and Religion," because to know what we are talking about,
in religion or any other field, we must base our discussions
upon clearly discriminated metaphysical concepts.[15]

*Critical Remarks.* Whitehead's thesis about the significance
of Plato is the most aggressive one with which we are deal-

ing. Dewey, in fact, criticizes him essentially for his Platonism: his "excessive piety" towards Plato, his rationalism, and his conversion of moral idealism into "ontological idealism or spiritualism."[16] The first criticism is justified to the extent that no one should turn to Whitehead for a reliable historical exposition of Platonism. However, the originality and depth of Whitehead's discussions of Plato have the merit of rescuing important aspects of Plationism from neglect by showing their affinity with contemporary philosophical conceptions.

Whitehead and Santayana are at opposite poles on the question of Plato's most significant predecessor. While neither gives sufficient attention to Heraclitus, Cratylus, and Parmenides, Santayana emphasizes the Socratic, and Whitehead the Pythagorean, contribution to Plato's thought. Although Whitehead rightly emphasizes the rationalistic, Pythagorean roots of Plato's thought, he contradicts himself on the subject. Thus he says that Plato played the two roles of mystic and artist, and mathematician, and that in the former he "represented the world he inherited and not the world he created."[17] Like Taylor, Whitehead emphasizes *Epistle* VII, 341c, as throwing light on Plato's mental habits. But Whitehead's dictum that Plato's systematic thought is "nearly worthless" while his detached insights are "priceless" is a poor basis for interpreting Plato or his contemporary relevance, since there is no widespread basis of agreement to which disputants may appeal. Furthermore, to take Plato as a "mythical figure" and contrast him with the practical St. Benedict[18] is a distortion of Plato, since it ignores what the evidence of the *Republic, Laws*, and *Epistles* shows to be his concrete and practical interests.

Whitehead's assertion that his concept of an actual occasion is "little more than an expansion" of the first sentence of *Timaeus* 28a imposes upon that sentence more exegetical weight than it can possibly bear. Whitehead's actual occasions are the "really real" things in the universe, but Plato generally regarded the temporal world as deficiently real, compared to the eternal world. In dealing with the "final Platonic problem" of the relation of flux and form Whitehead is ambiguous. On the one hand, he says that in thought we inevitably presuppose a realm of forms (e.g., the multiplication table) in abstraction from the passage of Nature. On the other hand, "twice-three is six" is not tautologous but a form of process, since "the phrase 'twice-three' indicates a form of fluent process and 'six' indicates a characterization of completed fact." Both Urban and Dewey recognize this ambiguity, but on different levels. Dewey insists that Whitehead choose between a "mathematical-formal" and a "genetic-functional" interpretation of the world. To this Whitehead rightly replies that both methods are necessary. No star explosion generates the multiplication table by genetic functioning. "But such functioning does exemplify the interrelations of number." Urban presses Whitehead to choose between the temporal and the eternal as ultimate in metaphysical interpretation. If Whitehead were to do this it would destroy his philosophy. But because he cannot do it, his thought cannot be regarded as essentially Platonic, since Platonism generally regards the eternal as ultimate in metaphysical interpretation.[19]

Solmsen's view that there has been no revival of Plato's conception of Deity as a mediator between the sensible and intelligible worlds is contradicted by Whitehead's conception of the "primordial nature of God."[20] Although Whitehead rightly regards Plato's Psyche as the source of cosmic spontaneity, he erroneously identifies Plato's conception of the human soul with his own. Whitehead defines a person as a living society of high-grade mental occasions, supported by the low-grade occasions which permeate the body. In his earlier thought, Plato did not regard the *psyche* as a whole as a principle of integration, and *nous* was definitely separable from the body. And even in the *Timaeus* the *psyche* is not as organically related to the body as Whitehead thinks, since it is directly the creation of the Demiurge.

On the whole, it must be concluded that Whitehead's discussion of some of Plato's conceptions is stimulating and illuminating, if not sufficiently accurate, critical, or complete. Whitehead will not be remembered for his contributions to our knowledge of Plato; but after reading him it should be impossible to read Plato merely in the spirit of antiquarianism. It is a further deficiency of Whitehead's thought that he does not give detailed support to his contention that Western philosophy consists of a series of footnotes to Plato by illustrating the role of the seven notions more fully. His presentation of the Platonic tradition is highly arbitrary, as illustrated by his extreme emphasis upon the importance of the Christian theologians of Alexandria and his exclusion of Plotinus and Augustine from discussion.

Whitehead would deprive Christianity of its positive historical element by calling its Hebraic ingredient "barbaric" and sloughing it off. He assumes too easily that Platonism and Christianity are "congenial." There is no historical reason for regarding the Christ of the Gospels as the "exemplification" of Plato's divination that God is a persuasive rather than a coercive agency. In the first place, the more tender elements in the Gospel portrait of Christ are prefigured within the Old Testament. In the second place, a more complete and accurate portrait of Christ than Whitehead's would include harsh elements, such as Judgment, as well as tender ones.

*Whitehead's Constructive Religious Thought.* Whitehead seeks to expose difficulties into which three important human pursuits have fallen: the isolation of science, the irrelevance of religion, and the ineffectuality of philosophy.

"Philosophy asks the simple question, What is it all about?" This question can receive no final answer since human knowledge seeks to "express the infinity of the universe in terms of the limitations of language." The exactness of scientific propositions is a "fake," since even in logic agreement among logicians is by no means universal. But complete scepticism is self-destructive. Both the possibility of philosophical achievement and the inevitable difficulties of philosophy arise from the fact that "the mentality . . . and the language of mankind created each other." Platonic realism shows that if we speak of the same thing twice we demonstrate that the being of that thing is independent of either act of speech, unless we hold that the acts of speech presuppose one another, or are presupposed by the thing spoken of. On the other hand, philosophy must penetrate beneath the apparent clarity of common speech. It aims at "sheer disclosure" and is hindered by forms of language which lag behind intuition. Thus philosophy has a mystical quality, since mysticism consists of direct insight into unspoken depths. But philosophy would rationalize mysticism by "introducing novel verbal characterizations, rationally coördinated." In the first place, then, philosophy's method consists of analysis, which evokes insight by rational hypotheses, and evokes sustained thought by direct insight.[21]

But philosophy also discusses analogy, or "connected forms with overwhelming relevance." This procedure reaches its highest form when exhibiting the fusion of analysis and actuality, which is the opposite of trying to show how concrete particulars can be constructed out of universals. The permanent value of the Platonic theory of knowledge lies in its aim to seek the form in the facts. By virtue of analysis and analogy Speculative Philosophy is made possible, which Whitehead defines as the effort to construct "a coherent, logical, necessary system of general ideas in terms of which every element of our experience can

be interpreted." Speculative philosophy has fruitful connections with science and religion. It is the supreme expression
of the use of Reason whose function is to promote the art
of life in an increasingly satisfactory way. The interplay
of authoritative fact and reason's elucidatory power re-
strains the vagaries of speculation. Nevertheless, cosmology,
the most general form of speculation, is the rightful critic of
all more special forms of thought.[22]

Both science and philosophy are concerned with the relation of general principles to particular data. The field of
science is comprised of the observational and conceptual
orders of experience. The former is always interpreted in
terms of notions supplied by the latter. Speculative thought
must question the subjective order of prominence in which
science arranges facts, discriminate between facts as they
are and as they appear, and recover unwarrantedly dis-
carded facts. Cosmology urges the special sciences beyond
their pretense of finality. While in the past science and
philosophy have been mutually fructifying, in the present
philosophy fails to claim its proper generality, while the
sciences have become narrow and obscurantist. Perhaps the
time is not ripe for a *rapprochement* between speculative
thought and scientific method; but science has no basis for
this opinion, if it involves the depreciation of speculation.
For speculative thought is a source of evidence which it
would be irrational to reject.[28]

It is in terms of "ultimate rationalism" that science and
philosophy are most closely connected with religion. Philosophy gains its chief importance by rationally fusing religion and science. On the other hand, the faith and hope of
rationalism that every element of experience may be exhibited as an example of a general theory depends upon an
ultimate moral and religious intuition into the nature of
intellectual activity. Science would be impossible without
a widespread and profound belief in an order of Nature.

Modern science's faith in rationality must be attributed to its inheritance from medieval thought of a God conceived in terms of Hebraic dynamism and Greek rationalism. Again, since Christianity sought a metaphysics by demanding an intellectual justification of brute experience, "scientific interest is only a variant form of religious interest." However, in the modern era the relation of science and religion has been one of conflict because science seeks to harmonize rational thought with *percepta* themselves, while religion seeks to harmonize rational thought with "the sensitive relation to the percepta from which experience originates." Religion is essentially concerned with moral and aesthetic values, and science with general laws regulating physical phenomena. But it would be intolerable to acquiesce in this conflict because that would commit man to an ultimate irrationalism.[24]

Religion recognizes that human life consists of more than transient phenomena because it includes value. Religion not only mediates faith in rationalism but is also an important source of evidence for philosophy, since it presents the basic theme of divine immanence which completes cosmological speculation. Philosophy is indispensable to religion because the latter involves peculiarly complex patterns of emotion and belief which must be rationally understood. In the most famous of his definitions of religion, Whitehead says that it is "what an individual does with his own solitariness." This view directly negates the theory that religion is primarily a social fact, and that the purpose of religion is to sanction the desire for "a comfortable organization of society." Ideally, religion should be the basis of the unity of civilization, but it is only in an era of decadence that a religion is primarily social in emphasis.[25]

The main features discernible in the historical emergence of a religion are ritual, emotion, belief, and rationalization. Myth, for example, satisfies the demands of budding rationality by explaining the purpose of ritual. However crude the resulting concepts may be they do creatively advance rationality by stretching the mind beyond immediate sense perception. When it is fully developed a rational religion is essentially a metaphysics of value, holding that "the world is a mutually adjusted disposition of things, issuing in value for its own sake." Religious dogmas are general propositions, identical in logical form with scientific and philosophical doctrines. While dogmas may be false or static, they are necessary if religion is to be safeguarded against superstition. At the same time, the importance of rational religion is based upon its position that man knows more than can be formulated in any one "finite systematized scheme of abstractions."[26]

Although rational religion originates in the generality of thought which is possible only in solitariness, it subsequently passes over into "world-loyalty." In its solitariness the spirit is concerned with the value of an individual for itself, the value of the plurality of individuals for each other, and the value of the objective world which is a community derived from the individuals and at the same time the ground of their existence. Since the world manifests individuality in community, religion is concerned with that topic. And since the solitary has no value apart from the community of individuals, a transition to world-loyalty is required. Thus religion, through theology, is directly related to metaphysical description.[27]

Whitehead holds that it is necessary to construct an organic realism because of the prevalence of the fallacy of the "bifurcation of nature." Inspection of nature discloses things which flow, recur, or endure. To describe these things and their relations is the main problem of metaphysics. The most fundamental contrast in nature is that between Value and Existence. When this contrast is made into an opposition, there arises the familiar conflict between Materialism and

Idealism. The basic notion of Materialism is that of a "vacuous material existence with passive endurance, with primary individual attributes, and with accidental adventures." Exclusive adherence to this notion gives rise to the "Fallacy of Misplaced Concreteness," as illustrated in the Newtonian doctrine of "simple location." In contemporary thought men inconsistently combine a mechanistic materialism with a belief in the reality of human freedom and values. Most philosophers, with the exception of Plato, have tacitly assumed in their analyses of experience that it was possible to grasp clearly and firmly the fundamental aspects of reality. This led to a highly abstract theory of knowledge in which the emotional basis of experience was largely ignored. But the subject-object relationship cannot be identified with the knower-known relationship because philosophic thought must be based upon the most concrete elements of our experience, and must aim to elucidate it directly. The presupposition of Primary Substance must give way to the more Platonic conception that "every entity is in its essence social and requires the society in order to exist."[28]

Organic realism is more satisfactory than the dualisms of Hume and Santayana because it can show the rational connection between a form and any occasion in which it participates, and thus provide a rational cosmology consistent with the discoveries of contemporary physical science. The notion of fluent energy "conditioned by 'quantum' requirements" requires the conception of a natural event in which value is identical with its "intrinsic reality." Shelley and Wordsworth, among other Romantic (and Platonic) poets, presented the topics with which a philosophy of nature must concern itself: "change, value, eternal objects, endurance, organism, interfusion." For example, science is primarily concerned with enduring organisms. Physical endurance is the "process of continuously inheriting a certain identity of character transmitted throughout a historical route of events." Such a conception provides the uniformity required for scientific generalization, and procures the novelty required by emergent evolution. Furthermore, mental occurrences are operative in the course of natural events. In fact, apart from the experiences of subjects there is simply nothingness. But this position is not merely "a revolt against dualism" because "throughout the universe there reigns the union of opposites which is the ground of dualism."[29]

In the *Concept of Nature* Whitehead observed that the *Timaeus* suggests the distinction between the general becoming of nature and its measurable time. Thus, nature directly exhibits passage or "the creative force of existence which has no narrow ledge of definite instantaneous present with which to operate." In *Process and Reality* this is called Creativity and is described as the ultimate principle, or universal of universals, by which the disjunctive plurality of the universe becomes a complex unity. Creativity is protean, and apart from its creatures, or accidents, is devoid of actuality. The creative advance produces a novel togetherness, or "concrescence" of entities; but it is not separable from actual occasions, since it is always becoming for or with a creature. Like other actual occasions God is a creature, the "primordial, non-temporal accident" of Creativity.[30]

The first of Whitehead's twenty-seven Categories of Explanation holds that "the actual world is a process, and that the process is the becoming of actual entities." These actual occasions are the directly observed *Res Verae* of nature and experience. All actual occasions are concrescences of hitherto disjunctive components into complex unities. Each is *causa sui* and as such its own ground and outcome—a "subject-superject." "An actual entity feels as it does feel in order to be the actual entity which it is." In integrating a process of feelings an actual occasion attains a final unity or "satisfaction." This self-realization through the attainment of value is the meaning of matter of fact, "the evaporation of all indetermination." When actual occasions are together in a particular way they constitute *nexus*, or "Public Matters of Fact." Each actual occasion is a microcosmic embodiment and representation of the macrocosm, and combines the fluency of concrescence and the fluency of transition. The former arises from the actual occasion's final cause in the form of its subjective aim towards its ideal; while the latter is the vehicle of efficient causation, in making the past which has not perished operative in the becoming of other occasions.[31]

Whitehead defines a "prehension" as an "uncognitive apprehension." It is the occasion's process of unifying itself through a "graded grasping" of other occasions and objects. A prehension reproduces in itself the general characteristics of an actual entity, refers to an external world through its "vector character," and involves emotion, purpose, valuation, and causation. The positive and negative species of prehensions refer, respectively, to the inclusion or exclusion of a given item with respect to a subject's "own real internal constitution." A positive prehension is called a "feeling," and any actual entity felt is "objectified" for a given subject. The data of physical prehensions involve actual entities, and the data of conceptual prehensions involve eternal objects.[32]

Eternal objects, or "Pure Potentials for the Specific Determination of Fact," along with actual occasions and their components, express how all other types of entities are in community with each other in the actual world. Eternal objects have a dual reference: with respect to the "publicity of things" an eternal object is a universal; with respect to the "privacy of things" it is a quality or characteristic. The primary characteristic of an eternal object is its self-identity. *Sensa*, the lowest grade of eternal objects, are "permanences recognized in events." Unless there were such entities knowledge would be impossible, for one could not refer to the same thing twice, nor compare events. Eternal objects may function generally or specifically with respect to an actual occasion. As a pattern, an eternal object is the formal cause of an event, while as a "shaper" it is a final cause. "The organism is a unit of emergent value, a real fusion of the characters of eternal objects, emerging for its own sake."[33]

The term which Whitehead uses for Plato's *methexis* is "ingression," which he defines as "the particular mode in which the potentiality of an eternal object is realized in a particular actual entity, contributing to the definiteness of that actual entity." Because eternal objects neither disclose nor determine their ingressions there is an ultimate ground for empiricism. One cannot know a certain color by merely thinking of it in the abstract. The doctrine of ingression is founded on the "abrupt realization" or "graded envisagement" of eternal objects by the synthetic prehensions of occasions. In this way the actual includes the potential in its make-up. "It is the source of error, of truth, of art, of ethics, and of religion. By it, fact is confronted with alternatives."[34]

The objective species of eternal objects function relationally with respect to actual entities and constitute the meaning of "a real physical fact." They are the Platonic Forms which express the theory of extension in its most general aspect. The subjective species of eternal objects refer to the definite way in which a feeling feels. According to the Category of Conceptual Valuation, a conceptual feeling is derived from a physical feeling. Conceptual feelings are the basis of consciousness, or the "concentration of attention involving increase of importance," and the basis of judging between truth and falsehood. Truth is defined as the "conformal correspondence" of appearance and reality. Since clear and distinct appearance is primarily given in sense perception, we can gain truth more surely with respect to *sensa* than abstract forms. "We enjoy the green foliage of the spring greenly," but mere number, for example, imposes no subjective form.[35]

Whitehead illustrates "non-sensuous perception," which is the primitive base of sense perception, by reference to our knowledge of our own immediate past. Against Hume he says that Time is not a mere generic notion derived from "Presentational Immediacy" but that it is known in terms of "Causal Efficacy" or the succession of our acts of experience in which the consequent state conforms to the antecedent from which it was derived. The physical flux is continuous but it is an inheritance from individual occasions. Physical energy, then, is "an abstraction from the complex energy, emotional and purposeful, inherent in the subjective form of the final synthesis in which each occasion completes itself." However, human personality cannot be reduced to a genetic relation between occasions of experience, because personal unity is an inescapable fact. The human body is a complex of occasions which pours its inheritance into various regions of the brain. Against the Scholastic view that the mind "informs" the body, Whitehead holds that a "presiding personality" is produced by grades of occasions which are coordinated by their paths of inheritance through the body.[36]

The concept of personal identity is closely connected with that of human immortality, seen as a special topic in the wider theme of temporal fact acquiring the immortality of value. When a personal sequence can sustain among its occasions identity of value, the resultant value experience introduces into temporality an intimation of its own essential immortality. The survival of personal identity within the immediate occasion partially negates the transience of the world. Each occasion of a sequence carries over into the immediacy of the present the self-identity of its past.[37]

Whitehead's doctrine of God embodies the fundamental theme underlying his whole metaphysical position: the union of opposites. He aims to avoid the extremes of Oriental Immanence, Semitic transcendence, and monistic Pantheism. God is not a postulated exception to all metaphysical

principles but their "chief exemplification." Cosmology
may not reach the God worshipped in religion, but no doctrine of God is well grounded unless "the general character
of things requires that there be such an entity." While God
is essential to religious feeling by affording spiritual refresh-
ment and companionship, the "secularization of God's functions in the world" is an urgent metaphysical requirement.

God is the nontemporal "primordial superject" of Creativity which transmutes its indetermination into determinate
freedom. God transcends the Creativity by qualifying it,
and is transcended by it and all other creatures. God, the
temporal creatures, and the Creativity are meaningless apart
from one another. In *Science and the Modern World* God
is called the "Principle of Concretion" or limitation. Since
actual occasions are essentially emergent values, and since
value is dependent upon finitude, there must be an entity to
account for the nature and origin of actual occasions. Unless
the reality of actual occasions is denied, there must be
an ultimate limitation among the occasions which is the
"ground of rationality" and whose existence is "the ultimate
irrationality."[38]

The doctrine of God rests upon the "ontological principle" and the "principle of relativity." According to the
former, the reason why forms are realized, or are relevant to
the actualities of the temporal world, lies in their togetherness in an actual occasion. The principle of relativity, which
holds that every entity in the universe enters into concrescence with every other entity, also holds that "there can
only be one non-derivative actuality, unbounded by its prehensions of the actual world." This conceptual envisagement of the total realm of eternal objects and conceptual
adjustment of "all appetites in the form of aversions and
adversions" is called the "primordial nature of God." Comparable to Plato's Demiurge conceived nonmythologically
and to Alexander's *nisus* conceived as actual, it constitutes

the meaning of relevance. To be relevant, eternal objects must be compared, and God is the actual occasion which is the agency of comparison "for reasons of the highest absoluteness."[39]

However, in his primordial nature God is incomplete because his conceptual feelings lack complex integration with physical feelings. His "consequent nature" results from his "physical prehensions of the derivative actual entities . . . of the evolving universe." It is the world's reaction upon God, but it does not alter his primordial nature. Like all actual entities, the nature of God is dipolar. This concept of God explains how the universe attains "the active self-expression of its own variety of opposites." While there are many final opposites, such as flux and permanence, which are directly intuited as ultimate in experience, God and the World are interpretive concepts. Whitehead summarizes his metaphysics in terms of apparent antitheses which are actually contrasts. Thus God and the world are contrasted with respect to such polar conceptions as flux and permanence, unity and multiplicity, eminent and deficient actuality, immanence, transcendence, and creation. For example, "It is as true to say that God creates the World, as that the World creates God."[40]

The purpose of God, upon whose immanence the order of the world is founded, is the "evocation of intensities." Depth of value is possible only if "the antecedent facts conspire in unison," and consequently the order of the world is not primarily cognitive nor moral, but aesthetic. The world incarnates God as an ideal. However, like Plato, Whitehead acknowledges that the incompletion and evil of the world show that it contains formative elements other than God. Nevertheless, God meets each actual evil with a "novel consequent" which restores the disturbed harmony. Thus, Whitehead's view is like the aesthetic solution to the problem of evil proposed by Plotinus and Augustine. Evil is defined as "destruction as a dominant fact in the experience," whereas the good is inherently self-preserving. While the Good is identified with Beauty (which is the perfection of Harmony) there is an intermingling of Beauty and Evil due to the finitude of all actualization. Finitude is due to the exclusion of alternative possibility from realization. While the disharmony of Evil may be escaped through anaesthesia, by holding good and evil in tension, or by adjusting the intensities of incompatible feelings, Whitehead proposes a fourth way. In this way an occasion's spontaneity introduces a third system of prehensions which basically changes the intensities of the inharmonious systems. Thereby what is trivial as an immediate end becomes a suitable means for the emergence of a world which is clearly of intrinsic worth.[41]

Man's essential nature is defined by his conceptual entertainment of unrealized possibility, his "aim"; and he is directly aware of his purposes directing his actions. But man should aim at an enjoyment belonging to the process and not at any static result. The static maintenance of perfection is not possible; advance or decadence are his only alternatives. Therefore, Adventure must be included among the other ingredients of civilization, Truth, Beauty, Art, and Peace. Both Truth and Goodness are subordinated to Beauty. Goodness and Evil concern interrelations within the real world, while Truth and falsehood concern the conformation of appearance to reality. The highest type of Truth concerns "supreme Beauty," and is realized through a fresh penetration to the depths of reality. Peace is a "quality of mind steady in its reliance that fine action is treasured in the nature of things" and the "Harmony of Harmonies which calms destructive turbulence and completes civilization." It is a broadening of feeling which, like Grace, releases the self from preoccupation with itself.[42]

*Critical Remarks.* In support of his thesis that "abstract speculation has been the salvation of the world," Whitehead says that the final court of appeal for the truth of the notions of speculative philosophy is "intrinsic reasonableness." This might be true in a "civilized universe," but at the present time men not only differ about what is intrinsically reasonable but they also seek more ultimate courts of appeal ranging from brute fact to revelation. It should be noted that Whitehead himself appeals to both of these courts, under the names of "sheer matter-of-fact" and "the divination of wisdom."[43]

Whitehead is ambiguous on the important question of cosmic order. Having remarked that a religious intuition into the order of nature is the presupposition of scientific inquiry, he says elsewhere that order is a "mere generic term." There is only some definite specific order, and no single ideal to which all entities should attain. Whitehead gratuitously adds that the "notion of a dominant ideal peculiar to each actual entity is Platonic."[44] This half-truth ignores the role of the Idea of the Good in Plato's thought, as well as the aim toward goodness which characterizes the activity of the Demiurge and the "best soul."

Whitehead is more successful in his attack against the materialism and dualism of modern philosophy than he is in his effort to establish his alternative. By pointing out that there is an alternative to dualism which is compatible with recent developments in physics and biology, he shows the grounds on which natural processes and human experience may be regarded as homologous. But he spoils his thesis by overstating it, as when he calls value the "intrinsic reality of an event." In Platonism generally values are ideal realities extrinsic to events. The Platonic view that Ideas are "separate" from phenomena and that phenomena "participate" in Ideas is not as neat a theory as Whitehead's, but it accounts for the complex relations between ideality and actuality without confusing them.

Creativity plays a smaller role in Whitehead's thought than do the analogous concepts of *élan vital* and *nisus* in the thought of Bergson and Alexander. Whitehead's attempt to find an analogue to Creativity in the *Timaeus* is unsuccessful. Plato has a cyclical view of natural processes, and the Demiurge, the *paradeigma*, the *geneseis*, and the Receptacle conspire to produce aesthetic and rational cosmic order rather than novelty. Furthermore, Whitehead holds that the concrescence into which Creativity issues is known only by "intuition," although the production of novel togetherness is rationally analyzed in terms of its components.

Whitehead's ultimate "drops of experience" which unify the efficient and final causal aspects of cosmic process are analogous to Plato's *geneseis* in so far as they constitute the transitional aspects of process; but unlike Whitehead, Plato never puts his final causes *in* events. Where Plato harmonizes *eros* and *nous* to account for man's actual urge toward rational ideals, Whitehead's doctrine of prehensions tends to blur the distinction between fully conscious thought and the physical and emotional basis of that thought. Whitehead's eternal objects closely correspond to Platonic Ideas in being self-identical universals and formal and final causes. Whitehead agrees with Plato when he distinguishes between the two realms of actuality and ideality, but he departs from Plato when he says that these two realms are "intrinsically inherent in the total metaphysical situation." For example, Whitehead defines change as "the description of the adventures of eternal objects in the evolving universe of actual things." Plato could have accepted this definition, with the all-important proviso that change would be the adventures of "imitations" of patterns. Whitehead's doctrine of ingression applies the Law of Mutual Immanence to all things; Plato's doctrine of participation entails the position that no Idea is exhausted in any of its exemplifications.

Whitehead's doctrines of personal identity and human immortality also differ from the comparable doctrines of Plato. For both, the soul or self is a One and a Many, but for Plato psychic unity is not derived from the coordination of occasions of experience but from increasing knowledge of the Idea of the Good. Whitehead uses Plato's Receptacle (as the basis of Mutual Immanence) to account for personal identity and speaks of the grades of physical and mental occasions as "miraculously" coordinated.[45] This view is not only a distortion of Platonism, but it lacks the explanatory power which Whitehead claims metaphysics should have. Miracle is also brought in to explain how the multiplicity of the world of fact is transformed into the "coördinated unity of a dominant character," and thus provides a basic for immortality. For Whitehead immortality is inherent in the nature of things; for Plato it is inherent only in the Ideal and in that aspect of man's nature which knows the Ideal, *nous.*

Whitehead's religious thought has the merit of proposing a neglected theological alternative. The alternative presented by the *philosophia perennis* holds that the world is a derivative aspect, by creation or emanation, of God. The modernist alternative (illustrated by Dewey's giving the name "God" to the "active relation between the ideal and the actual")[46] regards God as a derivative aspect of the interaction of man and nature. In rejecting both theological absolutism and moral idealism, Whitehead holds that God and the World are mutually required aspects of each other, an alternative which is more consonant with classical Platonism and contemporary cosmology.

One critic makes a sharp distinction between the God which Whitehead derives from metaphysical analysis and the "God of religions," and holds that the religious qualities which Whitehead attributes to God have no rational foundation.[47] This criticism fails to recognize that Whitehead holds that the God of religious intuition and the God of metaphysical rationalization supplement one another. The enterprise of rationalism would be forestalled if it were not for the moral and religious conviction of God as the foundation of cosmic order, and the God of religion would be without relevance to the world if such relevance could not be rationally exhibited. However, the fact remains that one must accept Whitehead's metaphysics if one is to accept his doctrine of God. His "ontological principle" is within the Platonic tradition and it, or its equivalent, is necessary for a rational cosmology which proposes to account for the connection between ideality and actuality. The weakness of Whitehead's argument lies in the "principle of relativity"; for he does not show why it entails that there should be just one such entity as he describes God to be.

While the Demiurge and the Principle of Concretion have many similarities, Whitehead's doctrine of God as the foundation of the aesthetic order of the world is a distortion of Platonism. The Good of the *Republic* when taken in conjunction with the Beautiful of the *Symposium* is the foundation of the cognitive, moral, and aesthetic order of the world. In the *Timaeus*, the activity of the Demiurge is primarily the basis of the cognitive and aesthetic order of the world, and incidentally of the moral order. In *Laws* X, the "best soul" is primarily the basis of moral order, and its existence is inferred from the predominance of that order in the world.

Whitehead's "shift of meaning" which allegedly converts antitheses into necessary contrasts is actually a confusion of opposites which represents a fundamental divergence from Platonism. Thus, he says that the perfect realization of ideals is not merely the exemplification of timeless abstractions but that "it implants timelessness on what in its

essence is passing."[48] Whitehead merges the temporal with
the eternal, while Plato keeps them distinct. Furthermore,
Whitehead's emphasis upon the aesthetic order of the world
leads him to indulge in an optimism warranted neither by
Platonism, fact, nor logic. On the one hand, he acknowledges the Platonic "surd" in existence when he says that
"every fact is what it is," but on the other hand he becomes
pantheistically optimistic when he says that every fact in
"its union with God is not a total loss."[49] Whitehead sets
before man the ideal of perpetual recovery from the loss
entailed in process through his relation to the eternal. Plato
set before man the ideal of the achievement of an eternal
perfection.

# VI: Platonic Themes in Santayana's Religious Thought

GEORGE SANTAYANA (1863–1952) was born in Madrid, and came to America in 1872. He was educated at Boston Latin School and Harvard College, and lived in America until he retired from teaching philosophy at Harvard in 1912. The most influential of his Harvard teachers were Josiah Royce and William James. Royce was the first to perceive that the gist of his philosophy lay in the distinction between essence and existence. James's "radical empiricism" not only gave Santayana an appreciation of the immediate and contingent aspects of existence, but also guided him in the development of his doctrine of essences.[1] However, the Harvard philosophy department had not yet "discovered" Plato and Aristotle, and in 1896–97 Santayana studied them under Dr. Henry Jackson of Trinity College, Cambridge—a study which led to the production of the *Life of Reason*. It was also at Cambridge that Russell and Moore helped him adapt Platonic Ideas to his realm of essence. At this time Santayana found Plato the most attractive of all philosophers and, upon returning to Harvard, gave as his chief course a series of lectures on the great "middle" dialogues and Aristotle's *Nichomachean Ethics*. Santayana found that the principles of "orthodox" moral philosophy were set down in the *Philebus* and *Republic* I, and he traced this theme not only in the *Life of Reason* but also in the rest of his criticism of literature and religion. However, Santayana acknowledges that he treated Plato somewhat cavalierly and overlooked the profound and influential Pythagorean, cosmological aspects of Platonism.[2]

Santayana tells us that his earliest speculative thought was "philosophically religious" and that it has always remained so. A nominal Catholic, he has no apologetic interest in traditional religion, but at the conclusion of his greatest systematic work he transposed his realms of being into the Persons of the Trinity. The one is a language based upon analysis, while the other is a dogma based upon inspiration. Dogmas are not scientific descriptions of existence, but as the speculations of intensely consecrated minds their value lies in the aid which they give to the work of spiritual discipline in the attainment of inner harmony. "There they remain fountains of wisdom and self-knowledge, at which we may still drink in solitude. Perhaps the day may return when mankind will drink at them again in society."[3]

*Santayana's Conception of Platonism.* The main problem which Santayana sets himself in *Platonism and the Spiritual Life* is to determine the nature and relations of the two factors indicated. Although many things have passed for Platonism, it is essentially a whole made up of the thought of Socrates, Plato, and Plotinus. As an historical system Platonism is supernaturalistic, realistic, and dualistic, because it held that God and the Ideas are independent existents superior in every way to their earthly counterparts. When the Platonic system is taken literally and dogmatically it seems to be a "gratuitous fiction." But when taken inwardly Platonic doctrines are seen to be "the fervent expression and products of the deepest minds; . . . inevitable, persuasive, and morally coherent." Platonism has made valuable contributions to moral and religious thought. It shares with the spiritual life everywhere the gift of seeing the eternal in the temporal. It shares the classic attitude of reason in seeking not the mere continuance of experience, but its comprehension. Furthermore, Platonism is a genuine moral idealism. It was the earliest and best of all humanistic philosophies because it expressed the spiritual side of human nature. Platonic metaphysics was a form of poetry which projected the moral progress of the soul into the universe, thereby unifying and beautifying the life of the soul. Platonism was right in holding that the ideal is "something *better* than fact," but went astray in attributing "power and existence" to Ideas. A genuine idealism which consisted of thought and love fixed upon essence was transformed into a "gnostic physics" in which Ideas were confused with facts and values with powers. This happened because the mythical cosmology of Platonism had a parochial Hellenic bias.[4]

The central ambiguity of Platonism may be detected in the thought of Socrates. Socrates' moral philosophy was expressive rather than scientific, and his doctrine of self-knowledge held that moral truth can be found only after one discovers what he ultimately wants and loves. It was Socrates' distinctive achievement to transfer the attention of Greek philosophy from nature to art, and from life's sources to its fruits; and he became supreme in ideal morality, as Democritus was in cosmology. His Ideas were fundamentally utilitarian values discovered by a shrewd and candid reasonableness. His "logic of the autonomous will" is superior to ethical scepticism, ancient or modern. The essence of Sophism does not lie in the doctrine of a private seat of judgment, but in ignoring the ulterior reference of human aims and moral judgments, thus lacking an objective criterion of purposes. Socrates took these facts of the moral life into account, and further insisted that a rational examination and clarification of purposes should precede the selection of external means. But Socrates' achievement was marred in several ways. His assumption that human nature is single and immutable and that the soul is qualitatively

identical in all men is untenable. Again, there was a metaphysical side to his thought which consisted of the hypostasis of words and moral concepts into cosmic powers. As
*Phaedo* 97b–99c shows, Socrates was excessively rationalistic, for he would have imposed reason upon a universe
which is necessarily irrational. Finally, Socrates' fervid,
plebeian utilitarianism exhausted the good of this world,
and left nothing but "the immediate good of the spirit, the
naked soul longing to be saved."[5]

Plato's fame and influence has endured for twenty-three
centuries because of the "extraordinary adaptability and
vagueness" of his thought. Santayana regards Plato's Ideas
as the historical prototype of his own doctrine of essences.
At the beginning of the *Realm of Essence* he quotes *Timaeus*
27d to illustrate his distinction between essence and existence. Ideas and essences correspond in so far as both are
objective, self-identical or eternal, universals. They differ
in so far as essences are infinite in number, including all
qualities of sensation and all kinds of change or relation, and
are neutral in value and not confused with natural forces.[6]

When Plato distinguished between *nous* and *dianoia* he
meant that the former was "a moral faculty defining those
values and meanings . . . which took the title of reality."
In moral philosophy the hypostasis of the Good is thoroughly justified. Ideas as imperfectly imitated models express
man's moral nature attaining to self-knowledge and struggling after perfection. Plato's intellectual vitality and boldness encouraged him to substitute for real things the logical
distinctions which divide them, but the indiscriminate hypostasis of ideals is inimical to the life of reason. Hypostasized
Ideas were no longer regarded as values or "natural harmonies" presupposing the existence of natural beings, but
rather as the "underpinning" of values, or creative, substantial, and permanent powers. Technically, hypostasis is
based upon a confusion of formal with efficient causes.

This confusion depends upon the ambiguous use of the word "make." Ideas are only the final or formal causes of things. They are either the logical and aesthetic essences of natural things, or qualities and harmonies resulting from their concourse. The substance, genesis, and efficient cause of things lies in the dynamic flux of material existence.[7]

Santayana says that "half the troubles of philosophy" arise from the confusion of myth with moral truth. The myth which was intended as a symbolic substitute for an empirical description becomes an idol substituted for an ideal. Plato's myths not only stimulated speculative thought, but he distinguished between them and Ideas. With Taylor, and against Inge and More, Santayana holds that the Ideas were completely nonmythical. It was not until the time of Neo-Platonism that Plato's parables and allegories became "revelations," and "the master's counters, . . . had become his disciples' money."[8]

Santayana regards the general historical and psychological reason for the limitations of Platonism to be *politisme.* "To this descendant of Solon the universe could never be anything but a crystal case to hold the jewel of a Greek city." The early Plato, the poet and logician, became preoccupied with making the city-state secure and he became even less aware than previously of the infinity and contingency of existence. Religion became a matter of "moral education and police, and in no sense spiritual." And when Greek civic life lost its savor completely, the "post-rational" morality and supernatural religion of Platonism and Christianity easily prevailed.[9]

While Plato's philosophy ranks above Aristotle's as a work of the imagination, the Life of Reason finds its classic expression in the latter because Aristotle's sanity and sobriety is more faithful to the common sentiments of humanity. In his early thought, after dismissing Plato's God as mythical, Santayana suggests that Aristotle's concept of the divine is the most adequate in the history of religious thought. But later he says that the orthodox philosophical notion of God in Aristotle (and Plotinus) is also mythical. Despite the fact that Platonism seems to be more compatible with Christianity than the philosophy of Aristotle, this is not actually the case because Aristotle "does not undermine the needful contrast and interplay between the natural and supernatural as Plato does by rendering both poetical."[10]

Actually, although not intentionally, Christianity is, like all religions, a "moral fable." Its genuine greatness and beauty lie in its moral idealism, which is the basis of its historical fusion with Platonism. Both are markedly humanistic, and Christian Platonism is a deification of human morality and intelligence. While historical Christianity was a blend of Greek and Hebraic elements, Santayana holds that the latter component is more fundamental. Platonic Idealism is basically hostile to Christian orthodoxy which, in its forthright supernaturalism, shows how a religion may be morally effective. Christian theology and Platonic philosophy failed to harmonize piety and spirituality. Piety's object is the power on which life depends, but Christian Platonism posited other sources for life and welfare than those which experience shows to exist. Like Platonism itself, Christian Platonism hypostatizes values and fears the infinity and contingency of existence.[11]

Although Neo-Platonism was supernaturalistic, it could not succeed as a religion because of its rationalism and hypostatic idealism. Plotinus' thought was both subtle and systematic, but his foundations were less impressive than his results; and his religious thought was not widely accepted because it did not spring from the popular imagination and conscience. However, in Plotinus' "unclouded, synthetic, believing mind" Platonism "crystallized into the most beautiful of systems" which clearly exhibits the *telos* of spirituality. Plotinus defended the excellence of the material world against the Gnostics, but his view of nature was based on speculation rather than observation. Not concerned with explaining natural phenomena, he regarded nature as a stage through which man passed on his spiritual pilgrimage. Nevertheless, like Plato, Plotinus regarded the foundations of existence as material, temporal, and arbitrary.[12]

Santayana partially adopts Plotinus' concept of the *psyche* as midway between matter and spirit. But where for Plotinus *nous* is an emanation from the One, for Santayana spirit is generated out of the *psyche* which has been generated by matter. Unlike Plotinus' *nous*, Santayana's Spirit makes no return There, but "belongs here below." Nevertheless, Santayana holds that the function of the *psyche*, once having become spiritual, is to contemplate the Ideal. Another affinity between Plotinus' thought and Santayana's concerns the problem of evil. This problem, as traditionally understood, does not exist for the naturalist for whom nothing could be more natural than the conflict of many interests, powers, and ideals. Nor does it exist for the Platonist who knows that the Good is far away and that it did not remove itself from where it is absent. While we vainly search the *Enneads* for an explanation of the origin of evil, we may find there a clue leading out of "this natural labyrinth of evil." Plotinus' Good is the "mythical counterpart" of the moral harmony of the spirit. By the means of this principle Ideas were disentangled from the flux of experience and "consecrated, illumined, and turned into forms of Joy." This Joy, which is a release from evil, is the end of spiritual contemplation.[13]

*Critical Remarks.* Santayana's notion of the "Platonic system" is a distortion of Platonism. Platonism is simply not systematic in the sense in which Spinoza's *Ethics* is systematic. It is uncritical to suppose that the thought of Socrates, Plato, and Plotinus is a continuous stream, with no breaches. It is also uncritical to take a characteristic feature of Plato's earlier thought—the Ideas as "separate" from phenomena—and make it into the essence of Platonism. Plotinus, for example, held that the "intelligible world is not outside mind." Santayana's contention that "at bottom Platonism assigns all creative power to the magic attraction of Ideas" is without foundation. While both Plato and Plotinus regarded Ideas as *teleoi*—objective, ideal ends—there was no magic about their attraction. Rather it was a question of "participation." Furthermore, for Plato, creative power does not reside in Ideas but in *psychai*, which are the sources of spontaneous motion.

Santayana's discussion of Socrates' moral philosophy (following Jackson) is the most searching one which we have examined. He is free of what Cornford calls the "Taylorian heresy" of confusing the persons of Socrates and Plato, and of More's artificial schematism. However, he neglects the religious aspects of Socrates' life and thought: his mission, mysticism, *daimonion*, and conventional piety.

Santayana directly contradicts himself on the question of Plato's Ideas. On the one hand he holds that Plato confused them with natural forces, and on the other hand he says exactly the opposite.[14] However, he does put his finger on the major difficulty concerning Ideas as "separate." As extrinsic final and efficient causes, as hypostatized ideals, the Ideas tend to constitute a world behind the world whose connection with this world cannot be rationally exhibited. Nevertheless, Plato's Ideas are plausible not only as intrinsic formal causes, but also as objectively real ideals which are *ante rem*. Ideas, as Taylor and Whitehead clearly show, are *ante rem* as types and norms in moral and mathematical thought. As "real possibilities" or "pure potentials" no Idea is exhausted in any exemplification nor derived from any instance, since no instance fully embodies an Idea, but only suggests it. In this sense Plato and more orthodox Platonists than Santayana rightly regard Ideas as separate from particulars.

There is some justification for Santayana's stricture against Platonic *politisme* since even the *Republic* and certainly the *Laws* show that Plato was politically-minded, if not moralistic. However, Plato's thought is not as anthropocentric as Santayana maintains but rather cosmocentric, within the bounds of a finite, Hellenic cosmos. Furthermore, Plato's practical social concern is a permanently valuable feature of his thought, and should not be depreciated as a mere deficiency of spirituality.

Santayana is correct in seeing that Platonism and Christianity share a high moral idealism, and that the basic element of Christianity is its Hebraism. However, on this basis it is contradictory for him to call St. Augustine "a thorough Platonist," since he was actually the most Hebraic-minded of all Christian Platonists. In his discussion of Plotinus Santayana discloses one of the most serious of his inconsistencies in the interpretation of Platonism. On the one hand he holds that the Platonists substituted "the essence of materiality" for Matter, while on the other hand he holds that the Platonists needed and had a doctrine of Matter as temporal and contingent existence, in order that the Ideas might have a sphere of manifestation.[15]

On the basis of his materialistic presuppositions Santayana's interpretation of the role of the ideal and spiritual in Plotinus' thought is illuminating. But it has no actual historical foundation in so far as it makes the One "the mythical counterpart of moral harmony in the spirit." As B. A. G. Fuller points out,[16] naturalism is a fundamental ingredient of Plotinus' thought (as it is of Santayana's), and Santayana's euhemerism is gratuitous. Santayana's recognition of the importance of Plotinus in Platonism is superior to Whitehead's neglect of him. Unlike Inge and More he does not convert Plotinus into a Quaker mystic or a schizophrenic, but he almost completely neglects the contribution of Neo-Platonism to what Taylor calls a "thorough-going metaphysical theism."

*Santayana's Constructive Religious Thought.* It is the gist of Santayana's materialism that Matter is, not the only reality, but the only "substance, power, or agency in the universe." Matter is the "principle" of the flux of existence or nonbeing. There are two main objections to this view. The sceptical and empirical one points out that matter is not an immediate datum of intuition, and the scientific and logical one points out that no idea of matter can express what it truly is. Santayana meets the first objection by saying that real, material substance is the necessary postulate of all natural knowledge. In dealing with the second objection he says that the study of substance is properly "the study of physics," but it is not a physics which defines its atoms. Democritus, Descartes, and Newton with their graphic or mathematical physical concepts betray their Eleatic and Pythagorean ancestry. Matter is an infinite mystery, and all descriptive terms are symbolical rather than exhaustive of the reality to which they refer. In Platonizing physics, matter was regarded as a universal inertia upon which Ideas are imposed. But Platonism itself was protected from the consequences of this unrealistic view by an "equivocation" which held that matter was also a universal potentiality. By admitting flux Platonism permitted the particular exemplification of Ideas.[17]

In Plato *psychai* have self-motion and are derived neither from Matter nor from the Receptacle, but from the Demiurge or World Soul. Santayana holds that the Psyche is generated out of Matter. While genesis is ultimately unintelligible, Nature suggests that in matter there is a universal potentiality of mind. That consciousness emerges in animal bodies must be taken as a brute fact, although Behaviorism well describes the close connection between the mind and animal life. Santayana defines the Psyche, physically, as the "self-maintaining and reproducing pattern or structure of an organism, conceived as a power," and morally as what marks "the hereditary vehement movement in organisms toward specific forms and functions."[18] The Psyche is a "habit in matter" which generates spirit. Unless we acknowledge the material origin of the Psyche, we will fallaciously substitute spirit for matter in our thought. This "psychologism" has led to Berkeley's idealism and Leibnitz's monadology, as well as transcendental idealism, phenomenalism, and panpsychism. But the "latent materialism of idealists" is most clearly exhibited among the Platonists, and in German Idealism.[19]

Santayana makes Matter a surrogate for God, and in so doing appropriates the Platonic and Christian definition of Being. In the first place, Matter, as the source of all power and existence, is the proper object of reverence and natural piety. After denying that there are any necessary truths, Santayana uses Anselm's ontological proof for the existence of God and the Platonic definition of Being to set forth the distinctive characteristic of Matter as power or "the difference which the existence of one thing makes in the existence of another." On this basis there can be no question of the existence of an *ens realissimum.* The main question in dispute between atheism and theism is whether this most real power is better denoted by the term Matter or the term God.[20]

Santayana says that he does not separate essence and existence, but merely distinguishes them. Although this distinction was anticipated in the *Timaeus,* he thinks Plato was more concerned with the distinction between reality and appearance, and actually confused essence and existence by turning purely logical essences into dynamic agents imposing a given character upon existence. The resulting dynamic idealism has been Santayana's "bugbear" in traditional philosophy. The term "exemplification" expresses the fact that essences have instances, and applies both to the embodiment of essence in matter, and the disclosure of essence to intuition. "If I write the same word twice, the word which is the same is the essence and the words which are two are its instances." Matter is the "selective principle" among essences. The doctrine that essences are manifested tychistically rather than teleologically purges Platonism of its superstition. Nevertheless, the universe is not merely a congeries of haphazard events. The laws of nature are "tropes," or essences of events as distinguished from events themselves; and the reality of the laws of nature is expressed in the axiom of empiricism and the postulate of the uniformity of nature. The first declares that all events occur spontaneously and contingently, while the second declares that a spontaneous occurence will recur wherever similar elements are in the same relations.[21]

While essence and existence are not continuous, they are nevertheless "simultaneous dimensions of the same world." Like Whitehead, Santayana holds that the temporal is understood through the eternal. Where existence is vague and endured, essence is clear and thinkable, in being open to logical and aesthetic intuition. "The flux flows by flowing through essences." If essences were not traversed in all mutation, the parts of the flux would be indistinguishable, and there would be no order or quality in the world. Although essence cannot reveal itself or take on existence, existence is rendered determinate not only by antecedent events but also by essences as the norms of a given determination. Things, facts, and events are essence momentarily manifested or sustained in the flux of substance. Nevertheless, essences have no existential or ontological status; they subsist as tropes.[22]

The viewpoint from which Santayana criticizes natural science is that of "transcendental reflection," which has two phases: the sceptical, in which attention is directed to the immediate experience, and the assertive, in which objects of "animal faith" are defined and ordered for the purpose of intelligent action. While all sciences are relative, their object is in some sense absolute. The revolution from Newtonian physics effected by Einstein's theory of relativity shows that natural science discloses no ultimate secrets of nature. The forms of science are optional, like languages or methods of notation. Furthermore, this revolution does not mean that scientific materialism has collapsed, but rather the habit of clear thought and the power to distinguish accurately between the material and the spiritual. The cosmologies of Eddington, Jeans, and others are spoiled by their identification of the object of science with man's experience or knowledge of it. Such perspectives cannot be the ultimate object of science since many comparable points of view of Nature and external, objective points of contact with it presuppose "an absolute system of nature behind all the relative systems of science."[23] Although science is "but another name for consecutive observation and understanding," Santayana holds that no scientific system is to be trusted literally. Systems are valid only symbolically, and science, like theology, is "a form of discourse." Science expresses our dynamic relations with our environment. If philosophy and religion do not misrepresent these relations or contradict science, they properly express destiny in moral dimensions by the use of mythical and poetic images.[24]

In addition to Platonic Ideas Santayana finds affinities to his essences in Scholastic universals, and in the comparable doctrines of Whitehead, Husserl, Guénon, Proust, and others. Although Whitehead's eternal objects correspond to essences in their eternity and ideality, his doctrine of "scientific objects" is a materialization of the ideal. Whitehead has overlaid a relatively valid contemporary natural science with a highly speculative metaphysic. His doctrine of ingression overrationalizes contingent existence, and his hierarchical realm of eternal objects deneutralizes essences.[25]

While all approaches to essence are adventitious, the approaches through scepticism, dialectic, and contemplation are all equally legitimate and harmonious with each other. In laying the most emphasis upon the first approach, Santayana says that there is nothing indubitable except the character of some given essence. An essence is what is left of an object after it has been subjected to a thoroughly sceptical analysis. There is no question of belief in essences, for the intuition of essence comes after the suspension of animal faith and liberation from all anxieties of action. The intuition of essence is an *Anschauung* which may be either sensuous or conceptual. It is pure acquaintance with data, and as such the basis of literal knowledge. Dialectic abstracts essences from the object of animal faith and traces their inherent patterns, while contemplation is the sustained intuition of essences.[26]

Intuition is also cognitive when essences function as symbols in making possible a transitive knowledge of the material world which is "posited by" or the "first object of" animal faith. Transitive knowledge is objectively referent in two ways: it "leaps" by intuition to the consciousness of some given essence, and it leaps by faith and action from a given symbol to an existing object. Thus Santayana avoids the mentalism of British and German Idealism (which he persistently attacks) by holding that dialectic is concerned not only with ideal implications but that, due to its origin in psychic life, it has an existential reference. There is a distinction between essences which are intuited, and those which are signified or intended, such as *pi*. Intended essences are "better" than given essences, because they render transitive knowledge possible. No essence is a particular, but all are universals with logical or aesthetic individuality. They

may be either simple, like a given hue, or complex, like
Euclidean space. Instead of being arranged in a hierarchy,
all essences are primary. "The most agitated *Paradiso* ever
painted by Tintoretto, the most insane *Walpurgisnacht-
straum*, is as elementary and fundamental an essence as the
number one or the straight line."[27]
   Santayana calls the realm of essence as such "the texture
of our impressions." Its infinity is comparable to the modern
mathematical conception of the infinite series of numbers
which is "a perfectly exact concept or Idea, . . . with
eternally fixed ideal relations." The realm of essence or Pure
Being is anterior to all existence. Pure Being is essentially
the totality of distinguishable qualities; existence would be
impossible if it were not able to appropriate differing characteristics. Exemplifiable possibilities in the realm of essence
correspond to Whitehead's multiplicity of eternal objects
as pure potentials for ingression, but Santayana holds that
the realm of essence has no particular structure. It is a chaos
because of itself it is completely indifferent as to which of
its members should be exemplified. The only trace of structure which it has lies in the fact that it is impossible that one
essence should be another. Morally, Pure Being is that to
which spirit is addressed, and it may be likened to Nirvana.
But, since a perfectly free spirit cannot exist, essences become Ideals by entering into "an external moral relation
to the animal soul," when the soul happens to conceive them
or regards them as typifying the objects of its desires.[28]
   The realm of essence has an important bearing on the
realm of truth. Santayana defines Truth as the "standard
comprehensive description" of all things, comparable to the
mythological notion of the divine omniscience. With respect to this absolute Truth, there are relative truths, in conventional, moral, or dramatic forms. While there are no
necessary truths, denials of truth simply posit the unre-
ported truth. Thus, the Sophists' subjectivistic and individ-

ualistic relativism implied the unspoken truth that life was a treacherous predicament, and that they were determined to make the best of it. The realm of truth itself is the "tragic segment" of the realm of essence, or that part of it which is illustrated in existence and which is of momentous interest to the animal mind concerned with existence. With respect to conventional truth Santayana holds that, on the one hand, an "animal vision of the universe is, in one sense, never false," because it is based upon that animal's nature as stimulated by its immediate circumstances. On the other hand, from a transcendental point of view, such subjectivity is seen to be "normal madness," because a thoroughly finite experient assumes its perspective to be absolute. Dramatic truth is superior to conventional truth because of its moral origin, practical sanction, and moral synthesis of experience. Dramatic myth is superior to a Positivism which would reduce natural science to "pointer-readings," because Positivism would substitute the material instruments of science for the spiritual motive of science. A dramatic myth at least responds to the facts reflectively; a mechanical record of the facts is less cognitive and less useful. Like Whitehead, Santayana subordinates Truth to other values. It is the chosen object of the intellect, but the human spirit has other interests also. Like the mystics we must, in some sense, go "beyond truth." The spirit, in love and aspiration goes beyond the actual and yet not without "a constant speculative reverence for the truth in its divine immensity."[29]

Rational religion has two phases: "piety, or loyalty to necessary conditions, and spirituality, or devotion to ideal ends." A spiritual man lives in the presence of the ideal, whereby his material life becomes a transparent and mobile vehicle for the detached freedom of the spirit. Spirit and reason are not hostile but complementary, since it is the function of reason to judge the value and opportuneness of spiritual life in any of its possible forms. Religion, like poetry, gives a symbolic rather than a literal representation of truth and life. Both aim to express truly the nature of man rather than scientifically describe the universe. "Our religion is the poetry in which we believe." The worth of both lies in their appropriate expression of the meanings and values of life, and in their quest for ideal perfection. When unified in their highest forms, they enrich one another: poetry gives up its demoralizing frivolity, and religion surrenders its illusions. When religion has scientific pretensions it stultifies itself by confusing projected images with natural and social facts.[30]

Santayana bases his doctrine of spirituality upon naturalism, without recourse to traditional beliefs in a supernatural human soul or a precise divine revelation. "Spirit is nature's comment on herself, concise and emotional." Matter and spirit are not two worlds, but there is only one natural world. The spiritual life which is possible in this world "looks not to another world but to the beauty and perfection which this world suggests, approaches, and misses." Spirit is not a substantial power, but an awakening of the Psyche into pure awareness and actuality. It gives life because it constitutes the moral worth of natural life and describes it in terms of essence. Some of the terms used to characterize spirit are attention, fruition, and freedom. The difference between the material and the spiritual life is a spiritual difference, which lies in the quality of their attention: "the one is anxiety, inquiry, desire, and fear; the other is intuitive possession." Spirit regards not the infinity of Pure Being but finite being in its purity, simplicity, and truth, and thus enjoys aesthetic delight, moral peace, and intellectual clarity. Spirit finds, in its commerce with essences, that the immediate revelation of things is also their ultimate value. By means of spirit, experience is no longer merely instrumental to some ulterior end but rather self-rewarding. But this fruition is not a static achievement. Spirit is always open, free, and generous. It is capable of "tolerance of any dogmatic conception, and readiness to accept any kind of world." Spirit can regard all things with a joyful equanimity because of its "disintoxication" with the influence of values.[31]

The freedom of spirit does not lie in its power over the world, but in its impotence. It does not strive to change or possess the world, but seeks an "ideal dominion" through identification with spiritual values as such. The freedom of the spirit reaches its highest form in pure intuition which is the perfect actuality of organic life or "existence concentrated in the sense of existence." Sin and evil are distractions of, and burdens upon, the spirit's freedom. Pain is an example of the Flesh's distraction of the Spirit. Instability is an example of the World's distraction of the Spirit. Finally, the Spirit is distracted by the Devil or any internal enemy of spirit. This form of distraction appears in spirituality's defiance of piety in its delusive poses of omniscience and omnipotence. The Devil is best vanquished by the exercise of Greco-Christian humility—the sad and patient enduring of suffering.[32] Liberation is neither the fullness of the spiritual life, nor does it entail the denial of the spirit's natural source. No escape from nature and morality is possible. We may look beyond them, but we cannot get beyond them. The model of the liberated spirit is seen in the Christ of the Church's devotion Who is incarnate, suffering, and obedient, and Who returns "at every recollected moment, to perfect union with God."[33]

Thus, Santayana has an element of mysticism in his thought. Mysticism is a "normal disease" of the Life of Reason. In its vitality the Life of Reason contains the mystic's assurance and joy, but in its rationality it appraises the source and value of mystical assurance and joy. Santayana finds the basis of a critical understanding of mysticism in those Platonists who insisted that the end of mystical

union is the Good. In the *Symposium* the spiritual attainment of the Beautiful (or the Good) is partly based upon
the natural harmony represented by the ascent of *Eros.* The
liberated spirit seeks union not through a fusion of substances but through a "moral unanimity" with all natural
life so far as it is in harmony. But the Platonists and the
Fathers of the Church magically hypostatized the Good.
Hard facts are better spiritual guides than such a fable, since
they constrain the Psyche to live in harmony with themselves, and thus in harmony with itself.[34]

Having gained inner integrity, the spirit can come to love
the world with spiritual sympathy, or charity. Charity is
rational, spiritual, and humane; it is not the antithesis of
Eros, but "natural Eros enlightened." A perfectly free and
impartial spirit would be addressed to, and find its satisfaction in, an infinite and valueless pure Being and would find
that human morality is only "the inevitable and hygienic
bias of one race of animals." But it is inevitable that essences
should become ideals, or values for the anxious, finite human
spirit. Santayana defines value as something relative to actual natures, "a dignity which anything may acquire in view
of the benefit or satisfaction which it brings to some living
being." While Platonism's dynamic idealism must be rejected as mythical, its valid moral idealism presupposes a
doctrine of the Good as morally absolute. The Good is not
relative to opinion, but it is rooted in the "unconscious and
fatal nature of living things" which predetermines for them
ineluctable differences between what is good and bad for
them. The natural good of living things is unalterable so
long as they and their circumstances remain constant in
type. Finally, the Good is absolute in being "single and all-
sufficient, filling the whole heart, and leaving nothing in
the rest of the universe in the least tempting, interesting, or
worth distinguishing."[35]

*Critical Remarks and Conclusion.* When Santayana says that Matter (whether Democritean atoms or the human body) "plainly exists" he contradicts himself, and oversimplifies his topic.[36] For he later repudiates all forms of atomism because the nature and functions of Matter are mysterious. Furthermore, even his developed view of Matter is ambiguous since he holds, on the one hand, that Matter is *posited by* animal faith while, on the other hand, it is *given.* This latter position is more consonant with Platonic realism, which holds that Matter is a "surd." While Santayana rightly points out Platonism's equivocation about Matter, his own conception of Matter is more Platonic than he realizes. His view that "the intrinsic essence of Matter is unknown" is identical with Whitehead's Creativity as indeterminate, and Plato's Receptacle as formless. Furthermore, when Santayana says that "the great characteristic of matter as known to us is its potentiality" he closely approaches Plato's description of the Receptacle in *Timaeus* 5od, 52d: "From the point of view of origins, . . . the realm of matter is the matrix and source of everything; it is nature, the sphere of genesis, the universal mother."[37] Here again we have a characteristic of Matter similar to Whitehead's Creativity.

The weakness of Santayana's attack against "dynamic idealism" lies in the fact that his alternative account of the origin of the Psyche from Matter does not have the explanatory adequacy of the comparable doctrines of Plato and Whitehead. Broadly speaking, Platonism holds that only ontologically ultimate psychic factors in the universe can give rise to consciousness, while Santayana says that "the passage from vegetation to action seems to produce the passage from a dark physical excitability to the *qui vive* of consciousness."[38] Santayana is no clearer in explaining how Matter gives rise to the Psyche and how the Psyche gives rise to the Spirit than Plotinus was in explaining how *nous* emanated from the One and how the *psyche* went forth from *nous*. In this respect the *Realms of Being* are like the *Enneads* turned upside-down. Santayana's latent idealism appears when he makes Matter a surrogate for God and defines it as the power to make a difference. All the Platonists with whom we have dealt agree that *dynamis*, in some form or other, is ontologically ultimate. Santayana does not acknowledge, at this point, his dependency upon Platonic Idealism, and he oversimplifies the dispute between atheism and theism. When he attributes to Matter "all substance and power" he has a doctrine of "one-sided dependence" fully as absolutistic as those of Inge and Taylor. Whitehead's refusal to attribute "eminent reality" to either God or Matter presents the Platonic, middle-of-the-road alternative.

Santayana's balancing of the contingency and uniformity of Nature is thoroughly in line with the Platonic tradition. He is unacknowledgedly a Platonic idealist in endowing Matter with formal and teleological characteristics. Thus he holds that Matter is "predisposed" to assume a given form; that material agencies are "at hand, able to impose" forms upon Matter; that a "certain quantity of matter, already endowed with form," has "tensions calculated to change its condition." Thus, while explicitly repudiating any inherent structure or *logos* in existence which constitutes a cosmos, Santayana implicitly adopts it.

Santayana is not clear about the relation of essence and existence. On the one hand, he not only distinguishes them but separates them absolutely. "Existence is contingent essentially. . . . There is no necessary and all-comprehensive being except the realm of essence to which existence is irrelevant."[39] On the other hand, he brings essence and existence together as inseparable but distinguishable aspects of the same world. However, Santayana tends less than Whitehead to merge the temporal with the eternal, and in this respect is more faithful to Platonism.

Santayana's realistic view of Nature and mathematical conception of natural science is thoroughly Platonic, but his general position on science is not. He charges science with being unable "to lay bare the intrinsic nature of things" while he does not show how his "genuine physics," in preserving the mystery of Nature, contributes anything of value to a rational understanding or practical control of the material world. He departs even further from Platonism when he subordinates philosophy and religion to science, and then says that all of these disciplines are merely optional forms of notation. But if the forms of science are all optional there is no reason why science should be regarded as the test of the validity of philosophy and religion. Whitehead's view on the subject is much more Platonic and much more satisfactory, since all three disciplines are regarded as mutually fructifying and criticizing one another.

Santayana's doctrine that the realm of essence is "an eternal background of reality, which all minds when they are truly awake find themselves considering together," cannot be supported. Since essences are the self-identical distinguishable aesthetic and logical characters of existence, we can certainly have no knowledge of an essence not exemplified. The realm of essence does not prove, as Santayana holds, that Nature is contingent, but has the same value as Whitehead's multiplicity of eternal objects. Both doctrines point out that a significant understanding of Nature entails the contrast of determinate actualities with unrealized possibilities.

Santayana's view that there is an absolute truth is in accordance with Platonism, but his view that dialectical analysis of the realm of essence is merely an instrumental construction which is "not true, nor meant to be true," has no warrant whatever in Platonism. His realm of essence, unlike the realm of Platonic Ideas, has no intrinsic order which the appropriate method can unfold. Consequently, although the realm of truth is the segment of essence which happens to be illustrated in existence Santayana has no rational basis for holding that one system of thought more closely approximates the absolute truth than another. He even attacks the coherence theory of truth as self-complacency in thinking. But, as Whitehead says, a body of propositions must be clear and logically consistent; the propositions must widely conform to experience, and have methodological consequences.[40] If these criteria are applied to different sets of propositions it can be shown that one set is truer (i.e., more coherent in itself and with experience) and more useful than another.

Both Santayana and Whitehead attack a barren scientific Positivism which would deny any truth-value to moral or religious propositions. But Whitehead would preserve the relevance of religion by integrating it with philosophy and science; while Santayana would preserve the relevance of religion by assigning it to an autonomous ideal sphere. Santayana has the insight to see that both popular religious feeling and practice and profound religious thought are not necessarily connected with current sciences and philosophies. The truth lies somewhere between the positions of Whitehead and Santayana: religion must have a metaphysical reference, but its primary spiritual value is not dependent upon metaphysics. Religion is autonomous, but not exclusively so.

Santayana's conception of Spirit is too vague to be effective in the religious life of man. He says that Spirit is "roughly the same thing as feeling or thought; it might be called consciousness; it might be identified with the *pensée* or *cogitatio* of Descartes or Spinoza."[41] Furthermore, he never tells us why the purely contingent Psyche, immersed in a purely material flux, should give rise to Spirit which finds fruition only in being addressed to timeless, necessary, and ideal Being. Santayana's moral absolutism is similar to that of Plotinus and Inge, with the exception that the underlying ontological and epistemological structure is reversed. In Platonism generally the sensible world is derived from, and dependent upon, the intelligible world; for Santayana what is psychologically immediate is ontologically ultimate. As Russell points out,[42] it is difficult to see how intelligence can survive as a social force if Spirit is essentially a disintoxication with the influence of values, and a mode of disinterested contemplation. That view of Spirit is not consistent with his view of Spirit as the fruition of the moral life. Although Santayana attributes the rise of Spirit to Will, in its final form Spirit is actually "impotent." Finally, it is impossible to reconcile the conception of Spirit as impotence with the conception of Spirit as "pure actuality."

The chief merit of Santayana's religious thought lies in its originality and comprehensive, emancipating perspective. But it is also uncritically eclectic. His materialism and his idealism are not integrated, because he does not fully and rationally explain the connection between the two. That the flux of existence exemplifies essences ultimately just "happens." There is no reason why it happens. Another defect of his thought lies in his incomplete and inaccurate understanding of Platonism. While his partial adoption of Platonic Ideas as essences is sufficiently critical, he does not acknowledge his dependency upon Platonism at some other important points. His naturalistic interpretation of Platonism has no foundation in classical Platonism, since it consists of turning Plato and Plotinus upside-down.

The basic criticism of Santayana's moral philosophy, by Edman, Munitz, and Vivas,[43] that there is a radical breach between the "rational ethics" of The Life of Reason and the "post-rational morality" of The Realm of Spirit, is correct in so far as Santayana forsakes the cultivation of humane values for the contemplation of neutral essences. But there is a precedent in the Platonic tradition for Santayana's seemingly ambiguous position, and *Platonism and the Spiritual Life* may be regarded as the connecting link between *The Life of Reason* and *Realms of Being*. For Plato and Plotinus practice of the cardinal and civic virtues was a necessary preliminary to the contemplation of the Good or identification with the One. Santayana departs from Platonism in regarding concern with ordinary human values as hindering the attainment or spirituality. He preserves the verbal forms of the Platonic moral philosophy, but he does not preserve its serious practical intent.

On the basis of their naturalism both Santayana and Whitehead have shown better than Inge and More the essential connection between Christianity and Platonism. Neither is a Christian Platonist, but both show that Christianity and Platonism have moral idealism in common. This finding is compatible with the conclusion of Taylor and Temple that Christianity and Platonism also have ethical Theism in common. That Christian Platonism has consisted and should consist of at least these two essential factors may be regarded as established. There is little in Platonism or Christianity to contradict this conclusion, and much to support it.

# Conclusion

CONTEMPORARY PLATONISM is, in one important respect, a mediating type of religious thought. It acts as a spiritual and intellectual bridge between the past and the present. There can be no reasonable doubt that Platonism is the bearer of a permanently valuable type of religious thought. And it is equally necessary to emphasize that, except in the case of More, Platonic religious thought is not dogmatic, reactionary, or obscurantist. It finds the traditional conceptions of Platonism useful because contemporary religious problems require for their solution conceptions analogous to those continuously developed in the course of the Platonic tradition. Two examples will illustrate the freedom and reasonableness of Platonic religious thought. In Roman Catholic thought there is ultimately a sharp distinction between philosophy and theology, and philosophy is subordinated to theology. Revealed truth, the province of theology, quite definitely marks the limitations of any other form of knowledge, philosophical, historical, or scientific.[1] Even Taylor, who is most sympathetic with Thomism, is definitely Protestant in his thinking on this point. On the other hand, Platonic religious thought is incompatible with contemporary Protestant Neo-Orthodoxy which, for example, according to one of its leading proponents, denies the very possibility of natural theology.[2]

While contemporary Platonism is a mediating type of religious thought, it gains its distinctiveness, and its nature is expressed, through its treatment of recurrent and important philosophical and religious ideas. All of the Platonists whom we have studied (with the exception of More) emphatically concur that Platonism is concerned with metaphysical problems. All distinguish between essence and existence. For all, essence is at least timeless, self-identical Being. Superficial commentary is inclined to overemphasize this side of Platonism, an error toward which Inge tends. All hold that existence is contingent Becoming. Taylor, Temple, Whitehead, and Santayana have found this aspect of Platonic metaphysics illuminated by the thought of James, Bergson, J. Ward, Alexander, and others. There is more appreciation of the historical character of existence and less depreciation of the fluent world in contemporary Platonism than in the thought of Plato and Plotinus.

Like Platonism and Scholasticism, Existentialism starts from the distinction between essence and existence. But it differs from Platonism because it identifies reality not with essence but with existence.[3] Platonism could accept the Existentialist insight into the contingency of existence and the subjectivity of human experience, as Plato's allegory of the Cave, Santayana's "Animal Faith," and Whitehead's "prehensions" show. But the eventual irrationalism of Existentialism is incompatible with Platonism, which holds that there is an objective knowledge of the real world which is a reliable guide for human conduct.[4]

The basic metaphysical tension within Platonism concerns the question whether essence and existence refer to an ultimate ontological difference, or to an ultimate logical distinction. The *Timaeus* and *Process and Reality* suggest the latter, while the *Phaedo*, *Republic*, and *The Philosophy of Plotinus* suggest the former. In the *Sophist* Plato defined *ousia* as *dynamis*, or power to make a difference. With this contemporary Platonists (with the exception of Inge and More) would agree. What are commonly taken to be two worlds are brought together in Platonism in so far as it regards the historical world as a *genesis eis ousian*. But

Platonism has not achieved that ultimate harmonization of Becoming and Being which Gilson claims for Thomistic thought.[5] Rather it holds to an organic conception of the universe in which Being and Becoming are really distinguishable, yet really interrelated. Thus, while Whitehead wisely revived the organic realism of the *Timaeus*, his ultimate union of opposites is almost as un-Platonic as More's radical dualism.

In epistemology Platonism is essentially an objective idealism. The Ideas or their equivalents are not in minds or souls, but are envisaged by them. Santayana has the special merit of emphasizing the crucial problem concerning the separate existence of Ideas. Classical Platonism never formulated a satisfactory doctrine of *methexis*, as the *tritos anthropos* argument, among others, shows. As Aristotle points out, Platonism recognizes two *archai*, material and formal causes. All the Platonists with whom we have dealt accept the Ideas as formal causes. The revival of this Platonic notion in contemporary thought is a valuable contribution to the theory of knowledge. We must be able to use words, the meanings of which are universal, if there is to be any knowledge whatsoever.

As final causes, Inge regards Ideas as creative values. More's conception of the realm of Ideas is thoroughly confused. Taylor regards Ideas as logical and moral universals, teleologically ordered by the *ens realissimum* which is their ground. Temple regards the Ideas as a hierarchy of values, subordinated to the supreme value of Love. Santayana's position that Ideas as final and efficient causes are hypostasized values clearly marks one point of difference between an idealistic and a materialistic interpretation of Platonism. Whitehead achieves a more Platonic conception when he speaks of the envisagement of eternal objects in the primordial nature of God. However, he is ambiguous because he also speaks of ideals as "inherently persuasive." Santayana dissenting, contemporary Platonists interpret Ideas as final causes which constitute a hierarchy of real values, and are not mere ideals.

Since Inge and More largely neglect the problem of participation, there are two main positions represented in contemporary Platonism. Taylor, Temple, and Whitehead regard God as the agency which ultimately brings about the ingression of Forms into the temporal world. On the other hand, Santayana attributes the exemplification of essence to the contingent dynamism of the material flux. The difference between the two positions is that between a Platonic, teleological view of the universe, and an un-Platonic, tychistic one.

Taylor's comparison of Plato's dialectic with the method of the *Principia Mathematica* is suggestive. In Platonism dialectic is systematic inquiry into the first principles of thought and reality. In the light of Plato's dialectic, the scope of *Principia Mathematica* is too narrowly conceived. Although it aims at embodying the demonstrative rigor which genuine Platonic dialectic should have, Platonism aims at a "teleological algebra," and not merely a logical one.

Despite its rationalism, Platonism has perennially recognized the truth of empiricism in its doctrine of the surds of experience and of the transience and contingency of the phenomenal world. But contemporary Platonic religious thought is much more speculative and much less analytical than it should be. There is too much theoretical discussion, for example, of the ranking of values, and not enough open, patient examination of particular facts.

Platonism holds that in so far as a science approximates pure mathematics it is a genuine science, an organized and reliable body of knowledge. However, from Plato to Whitehead it has not regarded mathematics as beyond criticism, and some of its greatest contributions to knowledge have been in this field. Platonism regards mathematical physics as the most fundamental of the natural sciences. This is not only consistent with its traditional emphasis upon mathematics, but also with the actual historical development of modern physical science. The social sciences, unfortunately, have not developed according to the audacious vision of the author of the *Republic*. Platonic social theory is not the strong point of any of the contemporary Platonists with whom we have dealt. Temple's social thinking is the most vigorous and practical, but apart from his recognition of the importance of the Platonic principle of Justice, it is not essentially related to Platonism.

In connection with value theory, the term "existence" may refer either to contingent process or to essential being. Value may refer to the worth of that which is, or which may be. This interpretation is found in Plato's early dialogues and in Santayana's early value theory. Value may also refer to what makes a thing exist. This interpretation is found in Plato's Idea of the Good and Plotinus' One. Thus, within the Platonic tradition value has been regarded both as the correlate of existence and as the ground of existence. But Platonism has not held that existence is the efficient cause of the realization of value. In this respect the moral philosophy of Santayana is a radical departure from Platonism.

In ethics, Platonism takes the form of a rationalistic eudaemonism. It holds that there is a Good (as well as goods) about which man can gain reliable knowledge which constitutes his well-being or happiness. All forms of Platonism hold that man is free in the sense that he is directly aware of himself as a self-determining organism. Contemporary Platonism holds that man is determined by existence to a greater extent than either Plato or Plotinus held. This is especially true of the thought of Temple and Santayana.

Platonism is not a form of personalism because it does

not regard personality as an ultimate metaphysical category; yet it is not unsympathetic with this school of thought in so far as it stresses the value of the human self. Socrates laid great emphasis upon the *psyche*, or what Taylor calls man's moral personality. Ultimately, there are two different conceptions of the soul in Platonism. When Plato speaks of the body as *soma sema* he regards the soul as a substantial entity, a self-mover whose destiny is fulfilled when rigorously controlling, or divorced from, the body. However, in the *Timaeus* and *Philebus* a more organic view of the body and the soul is presented. Man's good is achieved not by escaping from the body, but through a harmonization of body and soul. Whitehead takes up the latter view, while Santayana definitely adopts an epiphenomenal view of the soul. Inge, Taylor, and Temple are inclined toward the first alternative, while More distorts it. Actually, the organic and the substantial views of the soul conflict. Depending upon whether one follows a naturalistic or a spiritualistic line of thought, one must choose between them. However, a reconciliation of the two views is possible if the personality or self is regarded as the reality which gives the body moral significance. More's supernaturalistic humanism is of little value for Christian Platonism because, as Temple points out, whatever else man may be, he is a natural being. Thus Christian Platonism can adhere to its Hebraic heritage and accept what the contemporary sciences of man tell us about him. But, as we have seen, Taylor and Temple fall into a natural-supernatural dualism of their own. Inge's objections to the atomic concept of the self were inspired by the exigencies of past polemics. As Taylor points out, unless we accept the concept of personal identity, there could be no moral activity or moral judgment.

Despite many affinities with historical religions and theologies Platonism is essentially a philosophy, a method of free, systematic inquiry into important problems, and at the same time a perspective in which those problems are regarded. Despite its affinities with various types of philosophy Christianity is essentially a religion, a faithful adherence to what it takes to be divine and the prosecution of the activities which this enjoins. It is not inevitable (as Inge and More suppose) that Platonism and Christianity be amalgamated. Each may do its work as independently as possible of the other. However, while Platonism and Christianity have never been thoroughly amalgamated, they have several important affinities with each other.

They agree in their ethical Theism. Both hold that God is good. Plato's criticism of the Homeric theology is a moral criticism which is comparable to the attack of the Hebrew prophets upon idolatrous conceptions of God. But where Christianity holds that God is primarily known in inner moral experience and in objective historical events, Platonism holds that God is primarily known as a rational inference from cosmic order (Plato) or in a rational, mystical experience (Plotinus). Nevertheless, Christian religious thought has incorporated these Platonic and Neo-Platonic doctrines. The thought of Augustine and Aquinas, the very types of Christian theology, illustrates this point adequately.

Platonism and Christianity agree in their moral idealism. They are both concerned with the best type of life possible for man. But Platonism's humanism is essentially cosmocentric, as the thought of Plato, Plotinus, Whitehead, and Santayana shows; while Christianity's humanism is essentially theocentric. The one holds that man's ultimate good lies in his knowledge of the structure of the cosmos; the other holds that man's ultimate good lies in the activity which is directed towards him by the agency which is the ground of the cosmos.

Platonism and Christianity agree in regarding Nature as ambivalent. For both it is a burden upon, as well as a vehicle of, the good life. But by reason of its fundamental theological tenets Christianity is committed to the doctrine of the goodness of the created world to a degree which Platonism is not. Finally, Christianity differs more sharply from Platonism in its recognition of the importance of history. The doctrine of the Incarnation certainly separates Christianity from Platonism, as Augustine pointed out.

The thought of Santayana excepted, contemporary Platonic religious thought holds that the relations between essence and existence can be explained only by recourse to the conception of God. Santayana accepts the ontological proof for his surrogate for God. Taylor and Temple combine the cosmological, teleological, and moral arguments and with Inge regard God as the source of essence and existence to which the cosmos is related in terms of one-sided dependence. More and Whitehead construe God as that whereby, in conjunction with other factors, the world is and has the character it does. More's dualism, which posits a refractory evil, entails a teleological argument which leads to the conception of a finite God. Whitehead's organic realism, which posits a world as necessary to God as God is to it, entails a cosmological argument.

Taylor and Temple regard theistic proof as a *fides quarens intellectum*, and Taylor has the best understanding of the nature of theistic proof in the Platonic-Augustinian-Protestant tradition. He points out that it aims to show that the prior theistic faith, for the sake of which the proof is essayed, is not less reasonable than atheism, and may be more reasonable. Of all the proofs offered, Whitehead's is the most original and impressive. However, it fails because he does not show that the world is a single aesthetic order, and does not show why there should not also be gods other than the Principle of Concretion. Rational proofs of the existence of God tend to elicit the very scepticism which they are intended to overcome. Religiously, the theistic proofs are idolatrous, for they assume that the premises of

the argument are more certain than the God whose existence is to be demonstrated. Belief in God is not the result of
a metaphysical argument, no matter how dignified its tradition or how bold its present development. Belief in God is
the product of the faith of the whole man, of which reason
is a part. The function of reason is to prune faith of its
vagaries, and to commend belief in God to sustained and
sober reflection.

The term "revelation" refers to God's self-disclosure to
man, and concerns the role of historical persons and events
as normative for religious thought. Inge evades the problem
through his eventual acosmism, while More's irrationalistic
dualism precludes a satisfactory connection between the historical and eternal. For Whitehead, Christian revelation is
the exemplification of previous Platonic intuitions, and for
Santayana it is an investment of humanistic value into a
mythical, but morally valuable, projection of an ideal.
Temple's distinction between "revealed truths" and "truths
of revelation" is of great importance, since it delivers Christianity from what Santayana calls "the fanatical defense of
fantastic dogmas." The most thorough treatment of the
problem of reason and revelation in connection with the
temporal and eternal is Taylor's. It recognizes that while
God's self-disclosure is the ultimate ground of the Christian
faith it must also be rationally analyzed as much as possible.
It recognizes that Christianity must accept the eternal and
the historical aspects of reality in their full and distinctive
natures, and yet also hold that they are reconciled in Christ.
Taylor acknowledges that this is a paradox which cannot be
resolved, but is rather a point of departure from which
Christian thought proceeds.

Every discipline, theology included, must trust its data
if it is to operate at all. On the other hand, every inquirer
must be careful with his data, recognizing that they are se-
lected from an infinity of data, and are envisaged in the

focus of a nexus of presuppositions. The data of natural science are perpetually accessible, and it is possible to achieve a large measure of precision, uniformity, and objectivity in dealing with them. The primary data of theology are those concerning the historical origins of a religion, which may be only roughly ascertained and confirmed. At this point there arises a great difficulty for Christian thought. It is an historical religion which regards certain historical persons and events as normative. But it is impossible to make a thorough rational analysis of an historical individual.

In view of this difficulty the question of mysticism arises. There have always been mystical and sacramental elements in Christianity. In Platonism generally there are two major kinds of mysticism. Acosmistic mysticism has some precedent in Plato and Plotinus, and is chiefly represented by the thought of Pseudo-Dionysius the Areopagite. In what Inge calls symbolic, objective, or sacramental mysticism, Nature is not regarded as a burden to be thrown off but as a symbol of an ideal world. This view has much precedent in Plato, Plotinus, and in Christian theology. On this latter view Inge, Taylor, Temple (and even More) substantially agree, although each has different emphases. Essentially Platonic mysticism stresses "assimilation to God," and has been widely influential in Christian thought and devotion. Neo-Platonic mysticism stresses identification with the One, and seems to be the special province of a few adepts. It is generally agreed that no form of Platonic mysticism deliberately courts irrationality. The Good, the One, or God is above reason in the sense of being richer than any rational formulation of it, and in being the ground of the rational enterprise itself.

The Christian Platonists whom we have discussed regard sin as alienation from God, but their discussions of the topic are generally superficial. Recent Christian Platonism has been too much a part of the "Genteel Tradition" with its elaborate theodicies and lack of realism. Temple's realistic social thought was not derived from his Christian Platonism, but from the course of contemporary events and the thought of such men as Barth and Niebuhr. At the present time the pessimism of the Neo-Orthodox theologians has greater factual warrant than the optimism of Christian Platonism. But this pessimism obscures Christianity's ultimate optimism. As Temple points out, Neo-Orthodoxy denies the Christian Platonist doctrine that moral progress consists of increasing conformity to the divine.

The problem of evil and conceptions of God necessarily involve one another. Santayana points out that for the naturalist there is no problem of evil, since nothing could be more natural than conflicts between various goods and interests. More's doctrine of a finite God arises from a dualistic solution of the problem of evil. Inge, Taylor, and Temple adopt the Neo-Platonic–Augustinian conception of God and the *felix culpa* solution which it entails. Whitehead adopts a finite God and the *felix culpa* solution. It must be admitted that theoretical discussions of this problem are not convincing. Nevertheless, the problem cannot be evaded. It is primarily a question of how far we can push our understanding of the problem in a way which is consistent with the rest of our thought.

In Platonism man's salvation and immortality depend upon his identification with what is eternal. In Christian Platonism immortality is an implicate of Theism. While the reasonableness of the doctrine may be demonstrated, immortality is essentially a gift to be appropriated by faith. Finally, Christianity has a doctrine of the resurrection of the body. Regarded symbolically this dogma corrects Platonism at one of its weakest points. It symbolizes the fact that it is the entire person who is to be made whole, and that salvation does not consist of releasing some favored element of man from difficulties.

It is our general conclusion that the Christian faith is not presented in its full vigor by the Christian Platonists we have considered, with the possible exception of William Temple; and that neither original nor traditional Platonism is adequately expressed in the religious thought of Whitehead or Santayana. Platonism has been connected with Christianity and Naturalism at the expense of some distortion of each of the three positions. Each position is, in principle, substantially independent of the other. Why, then, apart from a few clear affinities (and despite some grave incompatibilities) should it have been thought desirable to connect Platonism with Christianity or Naturalism? The answer lies, I think, in the persuasive fascination exerted by the mind and spirit of Plato.

# Notes

## INTRODUCTION

1. Maurice Nédoncelle, *La Philosophie religieuse en Grand-'retagne de 1850 à nos jours* (Paris: Librairie Bloud & Gay, 933).

2. J. H. Muirhead, *The Platonic Tradition in Anglo-Saxon 'hilosophy* (London: Allen & Unwin, 1931).

## I: THE CHRISTIAN PLATONISM OF W. R. INGE

1. W. R. Inge, in J. H. Muirhead, ed., *Contemporary British 'hilosophy*, First Series (New York: The Macmillan Company, 924), p. 190.

2. Inge, *Vale* (London: Longmans, Green and Co., 1934), p. 5.

3. Inge, *Outspoken Essays*, First Series, 1st ed. (London: .ongmans, Green and Co., 1922), p. 270.

4. Inge, *Freedom, Love, and Truth* (Boston: Hale, Cushman Flint, n.d.), p. 34.

5. Inge, *God and the Astronomers* (London: Longmans, !reen and Co., 1933), pp. 13–15, 100–102; *The Platonic Tradi-on in English Religious Thought* (London: Longmans, Green nd Co., 1926), pp. v–vii.

6. Inge, *Mysticism in Religion* (London: Hutchison's University Library, 1947), p. 47.

7. Inge, *The Platonic Tradition in English Religious Thought*, . 75.

8. Inge, *The Philosophy of Plotinus*, 3d ed. (London: Long-ians, Green and Co., 1929), I, 165–66.

9. Inge, *The Platonic Tradition in English Religious Thought*, pp. 69–70, 115–16.

10. Inge, *The Philosophy of Plotinus*, 3d ed., II, 231–32.

11. *Ibid.*, I, 137–38.

12. *Ibid.*, pp. 78–109.

13. *Ibid.*, II, 207–10. Cf. "The Permanent Influence of Neo-Platonism on Christianity," *American Journal of Theology*, IV, No. 2, 328–44.

14. Inge, "Origen," in *Proceedings of the British Academy*, XXXII, 7–8.

15. Inge, *The Platonic Tradition in English Religious Thought*, pp. 7–10.

16. Inge, *Christian Mysticism* (London: Methuen and Co., 1899), p. 78, Note 2.

17. Inge, *Mysticism in Religion*, pp. 90–104.

18. *Ibid.*, p. 100.

19. Inge, *Christian Ethics and Modern Problems* (New York: G. P. Putnam's Sons, 1930), p. 136.

20. Inge, *The Philosophy of Plotinus*, I, 72–76; II, 69.

21. *Ibid.*, II, 52–54.

22. Inge, *Mysticism in Religion*, p. 109.

23. Inge, *The Philosophy of Plotinus*, I, 10. Cf. "The Permanent Influence of Neo-Platonism on Christianity," *American Journal of Theology*, IV, No. 2, 330–33.

24. Inge, *The Philosophy of Plotinus*, I, 133–37, 196–97.

25. Inge, *Mysticism in Religion*, p. 109.

26. Inge, *The Philosophy of Plotinus*, I, 147–51.

27. *Ibid.*, p. 131.

28. *Ibid.*, p. 145.

29. *Ibid.*, pp. 161–84.

30. Inge, Introduction to *The Essence of Plotinus*, comp. by G. H. Turnbull (New York: Oxford University Press, 1934), p. ii.

31. Inge, *The Philosophy of Plotinus*, I, 202–17.

32. *Ibid.*, pp. 221–33.

33. *Ibid.*, pp. 237–48.

34. *Ibid.*, II, 20–25.

35. *Ibid.*, pp. 39–91.

36. *Ibid.*, pp. 108–22.
37. *Ibid.*, pp. 127–28, 184–86, 207–10, 239–40.
38. *Ibid.*, pp. 109–16, 159–60; *Mysticism in Religion*, p. 153.
39. Inge, *The Philosophy of Plotinus*, II, 143–63.
40. *Ibid.*, pp. 202, 248; *Mysticism in Religion*, p. 9.
41. Inge, *The Platonic Tradition in English Religious Thought*, p. 76; *The Philosophy of Plotinus*, I, 81, 109.
42. Inge, *Vale*, pp. 55–59; *The Fall of the Idols* (London: Putnam, 1940), pp. 250–51.
43. Inge, *Mysticism in Religion*, p. 103; *The Philosophy of Plotinus*, II, 126.
44. Inge, *The Philosophy of Plotinus*, II, 57–65.
45. *Ibid.*, pp. 115–16; *Mysticism in Religion*, p. 156.
46. Inge, *Mysticism in Religion*, pp. 13–14.
47. Inge, "Origen," in *Proceedings of the British Academy*, XXXII, 9.
48. Inge, *Studies of English Mystics* (New York: E. P. Dutton and Co., 1906), pp. 1–3.
49. Inge, *Christian Mysticism*, pp. 5–8.
50. *Ibid.*, pp. 111–22.
51. Inge, *Mysticism in Religion*, p. 73.
52. Inge, *Personal Idealism and Mysticism* (London: Longmans, Green and Co., 1924), pp. 94–105.
53. Inge, *God and the Astronomers*, p. 217.
54. Inge, *Mysticism in Religion*, pp. 43–48; *God and the Astronomers*, p. 217.
55. Inge, *God and the Astronomers*, pp. 174–210.
56. *Ibid.*, pp. 71–122.
57. Inge, *Things New and Old* (London: Longmans, Green and Co., 1933), p. 35; *Mysticism in Religion*, pp. 65–69.
58. Inge, *God and the Astronomers*, pp. 191–97, 300.
59. Inge, *Christian Ethics and Modern Problems*, pp. 78–80.
60. Inge, "The Permanent Influence of Neo-Platonism on Christianity," *American Journal of Theology*, IV, No. 2, 337; *Personal Idealism and Mysticism*, pp. 158–59.
61. Inge, *Personal Idealism and Mysticism*, p. 22; "Hope Temporal and Eternal," in *Faith and the War*, ed. by F. J.

Foakes-Jackson (London: Macmillan and Co., Limited, 1915), p. 107.

62. Inge, *Mysticism in Religion*, p. 43.

63. Inge, *God and the Astronomers*, pp. 209–10.

64. Inge, *Mysticism in Religion*, p. 69.

II: THE CHRISTIAN PLATONISM
OF PAUL ELMER MORE

1. P. E. More, *Shelburne Essays*, Sixth Series: *Studies of Religious Dualism* (New York: G. P. Putnam's Sons, 1909), pp. 17–18. For external biographical details, see R. Shafer, *Paul Elmer More and American Criticism* (New Haven: Yale University Press, 1935); for autobiographical details, see P. E. More, *Pages from an Oxford Diary* (Princeton: Princeton University Press, 1937).

2. More, *The Religion of Plato* (Princeton: Princeton University Press, 1921), pp. vi–vii.

3. More, *Platonism* (Princeton: Princeton University Press, 1917), p. 2; *The Sceptical Approach to Religion* (Princeton: Princeton University Press, 1934), pp. 37–38.

4. More, *Platonism*, pp. 54–55; *The Sceptical Approach to Religion*, p. 92.

5. More, *Platonism*, pp. 74–146.

6. *Ibid.*, pp. 164–87.

7. *Ibid.*, p. 232; *The Demon of the Absolute* (Princeton: Princeton University Press, 1928), p. 1.

8. More, *Shelburne Essays*, Eighth Series: *The Drift of Romanticism* (Boston: Houghton Mifflin Company, 1913), p. 269; *The Religion of Plato*, pp. 340–44.

9. More, *The Demon of the Absolute*, pp. 44–51.

10. More, *Christ the Word* (Princeton: Princeton University Press, 1927), pp. 256–59.

11. More, *The Religion of Plato*, pp. 114–49; *Pages from an Oxford Diary*, Paragraphs IX–XIV.

12. More, *The Religion of Plato*, pp. 88–126, 223.

13. *Ibid.*, pp. 202–59.

14. *Ibid.*, pp. 280–87.

15. *Ibid.*, p. 311; *Hellenistic Philosophies* (Princeton: Princeton University Press, 1923), pp. 244–47.

16. More, *Platonism*, pp. 177–88.

17. W. R. Inge, *Mysticism in Religion* (London: Hutchison's University Library, 1947), p. 102.

18. See A. E. Taylor, *A Commentary on Plato's Timaeus* (Oxford: Clarendon Press, 1928), p. 79, Note 1.

19. More, *Pages from an Oxford Diary*, Paragraph XIV.

20. More, *The Religion of Plato*, p. 176, Note 10.

21. *Ibid.*, pp. 282–302.

22. More, *The Christ of the New Testament* (Princeton: Princeton University Press, 1924), pp. 206–7.

23. *Ibid.*, p. 293.

24. *Ibid.*, pp. 86–87; *Christ the Word*, pp. 240–65.

25. More, *The Christ of the New Testament*, p. 292; *The Sceptical Approach to Religion*, pp. 159–66.

26. More, *The Catholic Faith* (Princeton: Princeton University Press, 1931), pp. 122–63.

27. More, *Hellenistic Philosophies*, pp. 172–258; *The Catholic Faith*, pp. 216–19.

28. More, *The Catholic Faith*, pp. 207–97.

29. More, *The Sceptical Approach to Religion*, pp. 1–25.

30. *Ibid.*, pp. 189–93.

31. More, *Christ the Word*, pp. 267–68.

32. More, *Platonism*, p. 236.

33. See Plato, *Republic* 508e–509b, 490b.

34. More, *The Catholic Faith*, p. 297.

35. A. E. Taylor, *Does God Exist?* (New York: The Macmillan Company, 1947), pp. v–vii.

36. J. H. Muirhead, *The Platonic Tradition in Anglo-Saxon Philosophy* (London: Allen & Unwin, 1931), pp. 415–18.

## III: THE CHRISTIAN PLATONISM
## OF A. E. TAYLOR

1. A. E. Taylor, Biographical Statement in J. H. Muirhead, ed., *Contemporary British Philosophy*, Second Series (New York: The Macmillan Company, n.d.), p. 271.

2. Taylor, "Theism," in J. Hastings, ed., *Encyclopaedia of Religion and Ethics*, XII, 261–86.

3. Taylor, "Ancient and Medieval Philosophy," in *European Civilization: Its Origin and Development*. Under the Direction of Edward Eyre. Vol. III. The Middle Ages (London: Oxford University Press, 1935). pp. 735–845.

4. Taylor, Memoir of W. G. DeBurgh, in *Proceedings of the British Academy*, 1943, p. 390.

5. Taylor, *Plato* (London: Constable and Company, Ltd., 1922), p. vi.

6. Taylor, *Plato, the Man and His Work* (New York: The Dial Press, 1936), pp. 25, 285, 503–16.

7. Taylor, *Socrates* (London: Peter Davies Limited, 1933), p. 48.

8. *Ibid.*, pp. 133–41.

9. Taylor, *Plato, the Man and His Work*, pp. 177–234.

10. Taylor, *Socrates*, p. 173.

11. Taylor, *Plato*, pp. 38–45; *Plato, the Man and His Work*, p. 190.

12. Taylor, *Plato*, pp. 47–48.

13. Taylor, "Ancient and Medieval Philosophy," in *European Civilization: Its Origin and Development*, III, 769–70; *A Commentary on Plato's Timaeus* (Oxford: Clarendon Press, 1928), pp. 62–63.

14. Taylor, *Plato, the Man and His Work*, pp. 504–16; *Philosophical Studies* (London: Macmillan and Co., Limited, 1934), pp. 91–150.

15. Taylor, *Plato*, pp. 56–57; *Plato, the Man and His Work*, pp. 285–94.

16. Taylor, "Science and Morality," *Philosophy*, XIV, No. 53, 43.

17. Taylor, *The Problem of Conduct* (London: Macmillan and Co., Limited, 1901), pp. 426–511; *Plato*, pp. 100–105.

18. Taylor, *Plato, the Man and His Work*, pp. 413–15.

19. Taylor, *Epicurus* (New York: Dodge Publishing Company, 1910), pp. 24–25; *A Commentary on Plato's Timaeus*, p. ix.

20. See Taylor, *A Commentary on Plato's Timaeus*, pp. ix–x;

*Plato, the Man and His Work*, p. 456, Note 1; "Dr. Whitehead's Philosophy of Religion," *Dublin Review*, CLXXXI, No. 362, 30–36.

21. Taylor, *A Commentary on Plato's Timaeus*, pp. 64–70.

22. *Ibid.*, pp. 75–82, 678–79.

23. *Ibid.*, pp. 134–35, 299–300; "The 'Polytheism' of Plato: An Apologia," *Mind*, N.S., XLVIII, No. 186, 180–99.

24. Taylor, "Theism," in J. Hastings, ed., *Encyclopaedia of Religion and Ethics*, XII, 262–63.

25. *Ibid.*; *Plato, the Man and His Work*, pp. 490–91.

26. Taylor, *Platonism and Its Influence* (New York: Longmans, Green and Co., 1927), pp. 113–17.

27. Taylor, "Theism," in J. Hastings, ed., *Encyclopaedia of Religion and Ethics*, XII, 266.

28. Taylor, *Philosophical Studies*, pp. 159–60.

29. Taylor, "Theism," in J. Hastings, ed., *Encyclopaedia of Religion and Ethics*, XII, 270–85.

30. Taylor, "Philosophy," in F. S. Marvin, ed., *Recent Developments in European Thought* (London: Oxford University Press, 1920), pp. 34-58.

31. *Ibid.*, p. 61; "Theism," in J. Hastings, ed., *Encyclopaedia of Religion and Ethics*, XII, 282–84; *Philosophical Studies*, pp. 402–10.

32. Aristotle, *Metaphysics* 987b–988a, 990b–993a.

33. Taylor, *Plato*, p. 31; *Plato, the Man and His Work*, pp. 51, 503.

34. Taylor, *Philosophical Studies*, pp. 366–67, 390.

35. F. M. Cornford, *Plato's Cosmology* (London: Routledge & Kegan Paul, Limited, 1937), pp. viii–x.

36. Taylor, *The Faith of a Moralist* (London: Macmillan and Co., Limited, 1930) I, 7–9.

37. Cf. Taylor, *The Parmenides of Plato* (Oxford: Clarendon Press, 1934), p. 159; *Philosophical Studies*, pp. 189–90.

38. Taylor, "Modern Philosophy," in *European Civilization: Its Origin and Development*. Under the Direction of Edward Eyre. Vol. VI (London: Oxford University Press, 1937), p. 1265.

39. Taylor, *The Faith of a Moralist*, I, 15; II, 376–411.

40. Taylor, *Does God Exist?* (New York: The Macmillan Company, 1947), p. 126.

41. Taylor, *The Faith of a Moralist*, I, 250–52; II, 212–19.

42. *Ibid.*, II, 43–107.

43. Taylor, "Back to Descartes," *Philosophy*, XVI, No. 62, 126–37.

44. Taylor, *The Faith of a Moralist*, I, 33–69, 360–74.

45. *Ibid.*, I, 72–77; II, 336–63.

46. Taylor, *Does God Exist?* p. 112.

47. Taylor, "The Right and the Good," *Mind*, N.S., XLVIII, No. 191, 274–301.

48. Taylor, "The Freedom of Man," in J. H. Muirhead, ed., *Contemporary British Philosophy*, Second Series, p. 283; "The Vindication of Religion," in E. G. Selwyn, ed., *Essays Catholic and Critical*, 2d ed. (New York: The Macmillan Company, 1926), pp. 63–69.

49. Taylor, *The Faith of a Moralist*, I, 168–207; II, 208–10.

50. *Ibid.*, I, 159–62, 222–39.

51. *Ibid.*, p. 281; *The Christian Hope of Immortality* (New York: The Macmillan Company, 1947), pp. 12–13, 71–72.

52. Taylor, *The Faith of a Moralist*, II, 125–37, 326–28.

53. Taylor, "Theism," in J. Hastings, ed., *Encyclopaedia of Religion and Ethics*, XII, 286.

54. See Taylor, *Does God Exist?* p. 120.

## IV: THE CHRISTIAN PLATONISM
## OF WILLIAM TEMPLE

1. See William Temple, "Theology To-day," *Theology*, XXXIX, No. 233, 326–33.

2. Temple, *Plato and Christianity* (London: Macmillan and Co., Limited, 1916), pp. 3–9, 26.

3. Temple, "Plato's Vision of the Ideas," *Mind*, N.S., XVII, No. 68, 502–17.

4. Temple, *Plato and Christianity*, p. 26.

5. Temple, *Nature, Man and God* (New York: The Macmillan Company, 1949), pp. 82–108.

6. Temple, *Mens Creatrix* (London: Macmillan and Co., Limited, 1923), p. 65.

7. Temple, *Plato and Christianity*, p. 12.

8. Temple, "Symbolism as a Metaphysical Principle," *Mind*, N.S., XXXI, No. 124, 474.

9. Temple, *Nature, Man and God*, pp. 110, 487–90.

10. Temple, *Plato and Christianity*, pp. 31–39, 72–74, 90–91.

11. See Temple, "What Christians Stand For in the Secular World," *The Christian News-Letter*, Supplement to No. 198 (December 28, 1943), pp. 10–12; *Nature, Man and God*, p. 414; *The Hope of a New World* (New York: The Macmillan Company, 1943), pp. 66–67.

12. Cf. Temple, *Plato and Christianity*, pp. 42–51; A. E. Taylor, Critical Notice of William Temple, *Mens Creatrix*, *Mind*, N.S., XXVII, No. 106, 208–34.

13. Temple, *Plato and Christianity*, pp. 34–39, 72.

14. Temple, "Plato's Vision of Ideas," *Mind*, N.S., XVII, No. 68, 502; *Nature, Man and God*, pp. 362–67, 514.

15. Temple, *Church and Nation* (London: Macmillan and Co., Limited, 1915), pp. 149–50.

16. Temple, *Plato and Christianity*, pp. 28–30, 83–87; *Readings in St. John's Gospel*, First Series (London: Macmillan and Co., Limited, 1939), pp. 17–18.

17. Temple, *Nature, Man and God*, pp. 434–35.

18. Temple, *Plato and Christianity*, pp. 73–83; *Nature, Man and God*, p. 363, Note 1; pp. 457–63.

19. Temple, *Plato and Christianity*, pp. 92–96.

20. A. E. Taylor, "Note on 'Plato's Vision of the Ideas,' " *Mind*, N.S., XVIII, No. 69, 118–24.

21. See Temple, *Plato and Christianity*, pp. 20–22.

22. Cf. Temple, *Mens Creatrix*, pp. 211–13; *Christ the Truth* (New York: The Macmillan Company, 1924), p. 33, Note 1; A. E. Taylor, Critical Notice of *Mens Creatrix*, *Mind*, N.S., XXVII, No. 106, 224.

23. A. E. Taylor, "Truth and Consequences," *Mind*, N.S., XV, No. 57, 81–93.

24. Cf. Temple, *Plato and Christianity*, p. 88; "Principles or Ideals?" *The Pilgrim*, III, No. 2, 220–21.

25. See Temple, *Plato and Christianity*, pp. 93–102.

26. Temple, *Nature, Man and God*, p. 435.

27. *Ibid.*, pp. 18–56.

28. *Ibid.*, pp. 217, 256, 475–91; *The Nature of Personality* (London: Macmillan and Co., Limited, 1915), pp. xi–xxxii, 3.

29. Temple, "Some Implications of Theism," in J. H. Muirhead, ed., *Contemporary British Philosophy*, First Series (New York: The Macmillan Company, 1924), p. 420; "Symbolism as a Metaphysical Principle," *Mind*, N.S., XXXI, No. 124, 466–69; *Nature, Man and God*, pp. 481–93.

30. Temple, *Nature, Man and God*, pp. 111–30, 198–99.

31. Temple, "Symbolism as a Metaphysical Principle," *Mind*, N.S., XXXI, No. 124, 467–75; "Some Implications of Theism," in J. H. Muirhead, ed., *Contemporary British Philosophy*, First Series, p. 428.

32. Temple, *Nature, Man and God*, pp. 130–65, 201–19.

33. *Ibid.*, p. 250.

34. *Ibid.*, pp. 87–92; *Mens Creatrix*, pp. 31–72, 159.

35. Temple, *Mens Creatrix*, pp. 42, 125–29; *Christ the Truth*, pp. viii–ix.

36. Temple, *Nature, Man and God*, pp. 45, 193–94, 262–63, 475.

37. *Ibid.*, pp. 231–37; *The Nature of Personality*, pp. 8–20, 52–69.

38. Temple, *Christ the Truth*, p.33, Note 1; pp. 40–48; *Nature, Man and God*, p. 345.

39. Temple, *Nature, Man and God*, pp. 258–61, 283–84.

40. *Ibid.*, pp. 269–325, 396; essay on Revelation, in *Revelation*, ed. by John Baillie and Hugh Martin (New York: The Macmillan Company, 1937), pp. 83–123.

41. Temple, "The Divinity of Christ," in *Foundations*, by Seven Oxford Men (London: Macmillan and Co., Limited, 1918), pp. 211–63; *Nature, Man and God*, pp. 406–51.

42. Cf. Temple, *Mens Creatrix*, pp. 259–67; *Christ the Truth*, p. 303; "Theology To-day," *Theology*, XXXIX, No. 233, 331.

43. Temple, *Nature, Man and God*, pp. 164, 357; *Mens Creatrix*, pp. 262–86.

44. Temple, *Nature, Man and God*, pp. 244, 360–99.

45. *Ibid.*, pp. 467–68.

46. Temple, "What Christians Stand For in the Secular World," *The Christian News-Letter*, Supplement to No. 198, pp. 3–9.

47. Cf. Temple, *Christ the Truth*, p. 72; *Nature, Man and God*, pp. 514–18.

48. Temple, *Nature, Man and God*, pp. 165, 190–94.

49. *Ibid.*, p. 136; *Christ the Truth*, pp. 31–33.

50. A. E. Taylor, Critical Notice of *Mens Creatrix*, *Mind*, N.S.. XXVII, No. 106, 214–15.

## V: PLATONIC THEMES IN WHITEHEAD'S RELIGIOUS THOUGHT

1. A. N. Whitehead, *Process and Reality* (New York: The Social Science Book Store, 1941), p. 63.

2. Whitehead, *Religion in the Making* (New York: The Macmillan Company, 1926), pp. 63–64; *Science and the Modern World* (New York: The New American Library, 1948), pp. 28–39. 173.

3. Whitehead, *Adventures of Ideas* (New York: The Macmillan Company, 1933), pp. 124–26, 184–85, 213, 293; *The Function of Reason* (Princeton: Princeton University Press, 1929), pp. 6–8.

4. Whitehead, *Adventures of Ideas*, p. 203.

5. Whitehead, "Process and Reality," in *Essays in Science and Philosophy* (New York: The Philosophical Library, 1947), p. 89.

6. Whitehead, "Immortality," in *Essays in Science and Philosophy*, pp. 62–65; *The Function of Reason*, pp. 25–26.

7. Whitehead, *Adventures of Ideas*, pp. 53, 64, 188–205; *Religion in the Making*, pp. 41, 152–54.

8. Whitehead, *Adventures of Ideas*, pp. 84, 189, 298–99, 322–23.

9. *Ibid.*, pp. 142–56, 192–93, 271–72; *Process and Reality*, pp. 28–37, 146–47.

10. Whitehead, *Process and Reality*, p. 145.

11. Whitehead, *Adventures of Ideas*, pp. 40–53, 125–26, 190;

"Mathematics and the Good," in *Essays in Science and Philosophy*, pp. 75–90.

12. Whitehead, *Adventures of Ideas*, pp. 166–70; *Process and Reality*, pp. 31–32.

13. Whitehead, *Adventures of Ideas*, pp. 211–14; *Science and the Modern World*, pp. 191–92; *Religion in the Making*, p. 57.

14. Whitehead, *Adventures of Ideas*, pp. 213–17; *Process and Reality*, pp. 519–26; *Religion in the Making*, pp. 70–71.

15. Whitehead, *Adventures of Ideas*, pp. 46–50.

16. John Dewey, "The Philosophy of Whitehead," in *The Philosophy of Alfred North Whitehead* (Vol. III of the Library of Living Philosophers, ed. by P. A. Schilpp; Evanston and Chicago: Northwestern University Press, 1940), pp. 659–61.

17. Cf. Whitehead, *Adventures of Ideas*, pp. 70 and 191.

18. Whitehead, *The Aims of Education, and Other Essays* (New York: The Macmillan Company, 1929), pp. 70–78.

19. Cf. John Dewey, "The Philosophy of Whitehead," in *The Philosophy of Alfred North Whitehead*, ed. by P. A. Schilpp, p. 660, and W. M. Urban, "Whitehead's Philosophy of Language and Its Relation to His Metaphysics," in *ibid.*, p. 327; Whitehead, "Analysis of Meaning," in *Essays in Science and Philosophy*, p. 94.

20. See Friedrich Solmsen, *Plato's Theology* (Ithaca: Cornell University Press, 1942), pp. 192–93.

21. Whitehead, "Analysis of Meaning," in *Essays in Science and Philosophy*, pp. 93–99; *Adventures of Ideas*, pp. 285–93; *Modes of Thought* (New York: The Macmillan Company, 1938), pp. 67–69.

22. Whitehead, *Process and Reality*, p. 30; *Adventures of Ideas*, p. 285; *The Function of Reason*, pp. 5, 64–70.

23. Whitehead, *Adventures of Ideas*, pp. 197–99; *The Function of Reason*, pp. 49–50.

24. Whitehead, *Process and Reality*, pp. 23–24, 67; *Science and the Modern World*, pp. 13–14; *Religion in the Making*, p. 24.

25. Whitehead, *Adventures of Ideas*, pp. 206–21; *Religion in*

*the Making*, pp. 16–17; *Science and the Modern World*, pp. 190–91.

26. Whitehead, *Religion in the Making*, pp. 20–33, 126, 142.

27. *Ibid.*, pp. 58–62, 88; *Adventures of Ideas*, p. 221.

28. Whitehead, *Process and Reality*, pp. 317–18, 471; *Science and the Modern World*, pp. 50–77; *Adventures of Ideas*, pp. 225–26, 379–80; *Religion in the Making*, pp. 107–8.

29. Whitehead, *Process and Reality*, pp. 215–16, 254, 471–81; *Science and the Modern World*, pp. 95–111; *Adventures of Ideas*, p. 245.

30. Whitehead, *The Concept of Nature* (Cambridge: Cambridge University Press, 1930), pp. 17, 73; *Process and Reality*, pp. 10–11, 31, 47; *Religion in the Making*, pp. 91–92.

31. Whitehead, *Process and Reality*, pp. 27–33, 228–29, 250–51, 321–40.

32. Whitehead, *Science and the Modern World*, pp. 70–74; *Process and Reality*, pp. 28–35, 354–55.

33. Whitehead, *An Enquiry concerning the Principles of Natural Knowledge* (Cambridge: Cambridge University Press, 1925) 2d ed., pp. 62–63, 83; *Process and Reality*, pp. 32–35, 443–44; *Science and the Modern World*, p. 110.

34. Whitehead, *Process and Reality*, pp. 34, 391; *Science and the Modern World*, p. 177.

35. Whitehead, *Process and Reality*, pp. 40, 416, 445–47; *Adventures of Ideas*, pp. 321–22.

36. Whitehead, *Symbolism, Its Meaning and Effect* (New York: The Macmillan Company, 1927), pp. 35–47; *Adventures of Ideas*, pp. 239–44; *Process and Reality*, pp. 166–67, 514–16.

37. Whitehead, "Immortality," in *Essays in Science and Philosophy*, pp. 60–74.

38. *Ibid.*, pp. 174–80.

39. Whitehead, *Process and Reality*, pp. 28–46, 73.

40. *Ibid.*, pp. 46–47, 518–31.

41. *Ibid.*, pp. 161, 517; *Religion in the Making*, pp. 98–99, 152–56; *Adventures of Ideas*, pp. 324–36.

42. Whitehead, *Nature and Life* (Cambridge: Cambridge University Press, 1934), pp. 69–70; *Adventures of Ideas*, pp. 343–73.

43. See Whitehead, *The Function of Reason*, pp. 64–65; *Adventures of Ideas*, p. 53; *Process and Reality*, p. 63.

44. Cf. Whitehead, *Science and the Modern World*, pp. 4 ff.; *Process and Reality*, p. 128.

45. Whitehead, *Process and Reality*, pp. 166–67.

46. John Dewey, *A Common Faith* (New Haven: Yale University Press, 1934), p. 51.

47. S. E. Ely, *The Religious Availability of Whitehead's God* (Madison: The University of Wisconsin Press, 1942), p. 57.

48. Whitehead, *Process and Reality*, pp. 513–14.

49. See Whitehead, *Religion in the Making*, p. 155.

## VI: PLATONIC THEMES IN SANTAYANA'S RELIGIOUS THOUGHT

1. G. Santayana, "Apologia Pro Mente Sua," in *The Philosophy of George Santayana* (Vol. II of The Library of Living Philosophers, ed. by P. A. Schilpp; Evanston and Chicago: Northwestern University Press, 1940), p. 497; *Persons and Places* (New York: Charles Scribner's Sons, 1944), I, 15–16.

2. Santayana, "A General Confession," in *The Philosophy of George Santayana*, ed. by P. A. Schilpp, pp. 13, 22–23; "Apologia Pro Mente Sua," in *ibid.*, pp. 543–45.

3. Santayana, "General Review," in *Realms of Being*. One Volume Edition (New York: Charles Scribner's Sons, 1942), pp. 853–54.

4. Santayana, *Platonism and the Spiritual Life* (New York: Charles Scribner's Sons, 1927), pp. 1–3, 17–19, 87–89.

5. *Ibid.*, pp. 21–22; *The Life of Reason* (New York: Charles Scribner's Sons, 1906), V, 240–43.

6. Santayana, "Three Proofs of Realism," in *Essays in Critical Realism: A Co-operative Study of the Problem of Knowledge* (London: Macmillan and Co., Limited, 1920), pp. 181–82; *Scepticism and Animal Faith* (London: Constable and Company, Limited, 1923), pp. 78–79; *Realms of Being*, pp. 30, 153.

7. Santayana, *Platonism and the Spiritual Life*, pp. 8–14; *Realms of Being*, pp. 385–87.

8. Santayana, *The Life of Reason* (New York: Charles

Scribner's Sons, 1936), III, 130–39; *Realms of Being*, p. 156; *Interpretations of Poetry and Religion* (New York: Charles Scribner's Sons, 1900), p. 78.

9. Santayana, *Platonism and the Spiritual Life*, pp. 27–28; *The Genteel Tradition at Bay* (New York: Charles Scribner's Sons, 1931), p. 44.

10. Santayana, *The Life of Reason* (New York: Charles Scribner's Sons, 1917), I, 20–21; *Interpretations of Poetry and Religion*, pp. 70–73; *The Idea of Christ in the Gospels* (New York: Charles Scribner's Sons, 1946), p. 62.

11. Santayana, *The Genteel Tradition at Bay*, pp. 6, 41–47; *The Idea of Christ in the Gospels*, pp. 190, 237; *Platonism and the Spiritual Life*, pp. 93–94.

12. Santayana, *Interpretations of Poetry and Religion*, pp. 78–80; *Platonism and the Spiritual Life*, pp. 23–26; *Realms of Being*, p. 390. It is interesting to observe that Santayana adopts as a motto for *The Realm of Matter* a sentence from *Enneads* I.8.14, and as a motto for *The Realm of Spirit* a sentence from *Enneads* III.5.10.

13. Santayana, *Soliloquies in England and Later Soliloquies* (New York: Charles Scribner's Sons, 1922), pp. 227–28; *Obiter Scripta: Essays, Lectures, and Reviews*, ed. by J. Buchler and B. Schwartz (New York: Charles Scribner's Sons, 1926), pp. 83–87.

14. Cf. Santayana, *Realms of Being*, p. 153; *The Life of Reason*, I, 194.

15. Cf. Santayana, *Realms of Being*, pp. 385, 390.

16. See B. A. G. Fuller, *The Problem of Evil in Plotinus* (Cambridge: Cambridge University Press, 1912), pp. 329–32.

17. Santayana, "Apologia Pro Mente Sua," in *The Philosophy of George Santayana*, ed. by P. A. Schilpp, p. 509; *Realms of Being*, pp. 48, 177, 185–86, 221–32.

18. Santayana, *Realms of Being*, pp. 569–70.

19. *Ibid.*, pp. 355–87.

20. *Ibid.*, pp. 191–92, 413–14, 838.

21. Santayana, "Apologia Pro Mente Sua," in *The Philosophy of George Santayana*, ed. by P. A. Schilpp, pp. 525, 544; *Realms of Being*, pp. 121, 293–302.

22. Santayana, *Realms of Being*, pp. 39–40, 305, 603.

23. *Ibid.*, p. 200; "Revolutions in Science," *The New Adelphi*, I, No. 3, 209–11.

24. Santayana, *Realms of Being*, p. 137; "A General Confession," in *The Philosophy of George Santayana*, ed. by P. A. Schilpp, p. 8.

25. Santayana, *Realms of Being*, pp. 170–71.

26. Santayana, "Three Proofs of Realism," in *Essays in Critical Realism*, pp. 181–82; *Realms of Being*, pp. 3–6, 646.

27. Santayana, "Three Proofs of Realism," in *Essays in Critical Realism*, p. 183; *Realms of Being*, pp. 115–18, 142, 165–66.

28. Santayana, "Apologia Pro Mente Sua," in *The Philosophy of George Santayana*, ed. by P. A. Schilpp, pp. 529–30, 545–46; *Realms of Being*, pp. 430–31; *Platonism and the Spiritual Life*, pp. 65–68.

29. Santayana, *Realms of Being*, pp. xv, 401–6, 456, 530–46.

30. Santayana, *The Life of Reason*, III, 157, 276; *Platonism and the Spiritual Life*, pp. 40, 60–62; *Interpretations of Poetry and Religion*, pp. v–vi, 26, 290.

31. Santayana, *Platonism and the Spiritual Life*, pp. 29–58, 83–93; *Realms of Being*, pp. 572, 833.

32. Santayana, *Realms of Being*, pp. 643–730.

33. Santayana, "The Prestige of the Infinite," *Journal of Philosophy*, XXIX, No. 11, 288; *The Idea of Christ in the Gospels*, pp. 250–51.

34. Santayana, *The Life of Reason*, III, 278–79; *Realms of Being*, pp. 771–78.

35. Santayana, *Realms of Being*, pp. 783–96; *Platonism and the Spiritual Life*, pp. 3, 12–14, 45–46.

36. Santayana, *The Life of Reason*, V, 100, Note.

37. Santayana, *Realms of Being*, p. 189.

38. *Ibid.*, p. 570.

39. Santayana, *Platonism and the Spiritual Life*, pp. 35–36.

40. A. N. Whitehead, *The Function of Reason* (Princeton: Princeton University Press, 1929), pp. 52–53.

41. Santayana, *Realms of Being*, p. 549.

42. Bertrand Russell, "The Philosophy of Santayana," in *The*

*Philosophy of George Santayana*, ed. by P. A. Schilpp, p. 474.
43. See *The Philosophy of George Santayana*, ed. by P. A. Schilpp, pp. 310, 215, 350.

## CONCLUSION

1. See Canon G. D. Smith, "Faith and Revealed Truth," in *The Teaching of the Catholic Church, a Summary of Catholic Doctrine*, ed. by G. D. Smith (New York: The Macmillan Company, 1949), I, 36.

2. See *Natural Theology*, comprising "Nature and Grace" by Dr. Emil Brunner and the reply "No!" by Dr. Karl Barth. Translated from the German by Peter Fraenkel. With an Introduction by John Baillie (London: Geoffrey Bles, 1946).

3. See Paul Tillich, "Existential Philosophy," *Journal of the History of Ideas* (January, 1944), p. 44.

4. See John Wild, *Introduction to Realistic Philosophy* (New York: Harper & Brothers, 1948), pp. 6ff.

5. See E. Gilson, *The Spirit of Mediaeval Philosophy*, trans. by A. H. C. Downes (New York: Charles Scribner's Sons, 1940), pp. 82–83.

# Index